U-BOAT PENS OF THE ATLANTIC BATTLE

PHILIP KAPLAN

Pen & Sword
MILITARY

For Neal

First published in 2018 by
Pen & Sword Military
An imprint of
Pen & Sword Books Ltd
47 Church Street
Barnsley
South Yorkshire
S70 2AS

Copyright Philip Kaplan © 2017

ISBN 978 1 52670 544 0

A CIP catalogue record for this book is available from
the British Library

Typeset by Philip Kaplan

Printed and bound in India
by Replika Press Pvt. Ltd.

Pen & Sword Books Ltd incorporates the imprints of
Pen & Sword Archaeology, Atlas, Aviation,
Battleground, Discovery, Family History, History,
Maritime, Military, Naval, Politics, Railways, Select,
Transport, True Crime, Fiction, Frontline Books, Leo
Cooper, Praetorian Press, Seaforth Publishing,
Wharncliffe and White Owl.

For a complete list of Pen & Sword titles please contact
PEN & SWORD BOOKS LIMITED
47 Church Street
Barnsley
South Yorkshire
S70 2AS

E-mail: enquiries@pen-and-sword.co.uk
Website: www.pen-and-sword.co.uk

Book design: Philip Kaplan

CONTENTS

The U-bunker at La Pallice, Brittany; top:
The white cap of a U-boat commander.

The massive turntable for re-directing submarines at Lorient.

THE BEGINNING

The early U-boat shelter structures, know as "pens" were designed and constructed during the First World War. They sat on wooden foundations and their scale and function was best suited to protect against aerial attack in a time when small, relatively light bombs were dropped by airmen over the sides of their cockpits. With the coming of the Second World War, air bombing technology had developed considerably, but the ability of Royal Air Force bomb aimers to find, attack and hit their targets in enemy-occupied Europe was still marginal.

As British aviation technology continued to improve, however, and larger, more powerful bombs and better navigation techniques were created; as the capability and availability of RAF bomber aircraft increased, it became evident to those in charge at the Naval Construction Office in Berlin that a pressing need had emerged for the design and construction of truly effective protective strutures to shelter the boats of the growing German submarine fleet from aerial attack.

The Germans had long been considering their needs along these lines and since Adolf Hitler had come to power in 1933, a fragile sort of general agreement had developed within the frequently feuding factions of the German Navy that such protection for the U-boat

fleet was had become absolutely vital.

Since the naval campaigns of the First World War, the *unterseeboot* or U-boat had been established as a key factor in German and other naval warfare strategies and tactics. It was the British Prime Minister Winston Churchill who would write of them: "Enemy submarines are to be called 'U-Boats'. The term submarine is to be reserved for Allied underwater vessels. U-Boats are those dastardly villains who sink our ships, while submarines are those gallant and noble craft which sink theirs." He also wrote: "Of all the branches of men in the forces there is none which shows more devotion and faces grimmer perils than the submariners," and "the only thing that ever really frightened me during the war was the U-boat peril."

Dangerous and threatening-looking, the submarines of the Kriegsmarine of both world wars had a genuinely lethal reputation from September 1914 when they went into action against three Royal Navy heavy cruisers and the submarine U-9 attacked and sank the cruisers *Aboukir*, *Cressy* and *Hogue* in one impressive action. The attack had been preceeded in August by one in which the German sub U-21 fired on and sank the RN cruiser HMS *Pathfinder*. These attacks were followed in October by one in

One of the Lorient U-boat berths as photographed in the 1990s, without water and sheltering a French sub.

A drydock at St Nazaire, Brittany.

which the U-9 sank the cruiser HMS *Hawke*, and on 31 December when the U-24 sank the pre-dreadnought battleship HMS *Formidable*. When you consider the reality of submarine warfare at the beginning of WWI, it is clear that the ability of the submarine to submerge and strike at a targetted vessel from underwater while that vessel had no capability to detect the presence of the sub (and no effective means of attacking that sub even if they could detect it), it is no wonder that enemies of the U-boats were clearly unnerved by the experience. Employing the torpedo as its main weapon, the U-boat was capable of sinking an armoured warship with a single shot. On the downside, while submerged, the U-boat was largely immobile and virtually blind. In that era, U-boats had little speed and only brief endurance and had to rely on relatively precise positioning before launching an attack on a surface vessel. While surfaced, a U-boat then was able to cruise at about 15 knots, less than the cruising speed of most warships of the day and only about 2/3 the cruising speed of most current dreadnoughts. For the rest of the war, the great British warships of the Grand Fleet, operating on zig-zagging courses and travelling at great speed, were fairly safe from the U-boats attempting to attack them.

But the actions of the U-boats shocked the British public whose navy was, at that time, the greatest in the world. In the course of that war the German U-boat campaign against the British merchant fleet nearly managed to bring the people of Britain to starvation.

In December 1906, U-1, the first *unterseeboot* to be built for the German Navy by Krupp-Germania, was commissioned. After that Germany's submarine strength grew rapidly. It led to a major arms race among many nations to design and build bigger, more powerful and better-armed submarines. Actually, it had been Germany's plan to send a huge fleet of cruiser U-boats to the American east coast, each boat with a 1,500-ton displacement and armed with a 150mm deck gun, six 20-inch torpedoes, and with a surface speed of 17.5 knots and a speed underwater of 8.1 knots. Each boat was manned by a crew of 46.

That plan was never implimented and the Allied victory in WWI with the subsequent Treat of Versailles, then banned Germany from building, buying or borrowing any kind of submarine.

Thereafter, research and development into submarine countermeasures began in earnest, with Britain focusing on her invention of the sonar detection system. Called ASDIC after the Allied Submarine Detection Investigation Committee, the apparatus transmitted a narrow beam of sound waves (which travel great distances through water and at four times the speed at which they

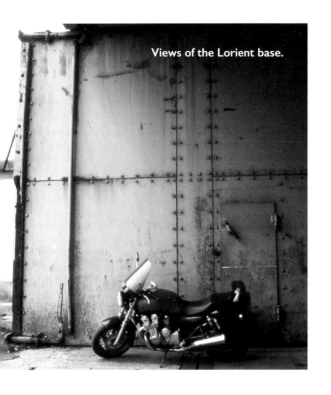

Views of the Lorient base.

pass through air) to sweep the sea around the potential target vessel. The sound waves produced an echo from any object in their path and the range of that object could then be calculated from the time interval between emission of the pulse and its return to the receiver.

ASDIC, however, came with many serious limitations of performance, not least being that it required a very skilled operator able to distinguish the echo of a U-boat from various other responses caused by fish, ocean debris, plankton, rough water, and even by sea layers of different temperatures.

The clear naval superiority of Britain over Germany at the start of WWI, and the subsequent establishment by the British of a naval blockade of Germany with the outbreak of the war in August 1914, had even food being seen as "a contraband of war". The Germans saw this move as an overt effort to starve their people into submission and there was little international support for this tactic. The inequality of British and German naval power meant that Germany's only effective means of countering that blockade was through the use of the U-boat, but there was considerable resistance in both Germany and the United States to the employment of such a 'shoot without warning' submarine blockade policy. And in November 1914, the British declared the entire North Sea a war zone. The Germans responded by declaring the waters around Great Britain

and Ireland, including the whole of the English Channel, a war zone. They stated that, from 18 February every enemy merchant vessel encountered in that zone would be destroyed, this despite the danger that threatened the crew and passengers. They further said that neutral vessels would also run a risk in the war zone as, in view of the hazards of sea warfare and the British authorization of 31 January of the misuse of neutral flags, it may not always be possible to prevent attacks on enemy ships from harming neutral ships. Over time this would bring neutral nations such as the United States and Brazil into the conflict. Soon, unrestricted submarine warfare was a reality.

In one of history's most dramatic ex-amples of submarine action, the British passenger liner RMS *Lusitania* with 1,959 people on board, was torpedoed by the German submarine U-20 some thirteen miles off the Old Head of Kinsale, Ireland. Eighteen minutes later it had sunk with the loss of 1,198 of those aboard, 128 of them American citizens. The incident enraged both Britons and Americans and the British urged U.S. President Woodrow Wilson to declare war on Germany. But Wilson chose to act by delivering a series of notes to the Germans in May, June and July. In the notes he affirmed the right of Americans to travel as passengers aboard merchant ships and insisted that the Germans abandon their submarine warfare against commercial vessels regardless of the flag the ships sailed under. In his second note, Wilson disagreed wih the German contention that the British blockade was illegal and a cruel, deadly attack on innocent civilians, as well as the German charge that the *Lusitania* had been carrying munitions. President Wilson issued an ultimatum to the Germans in his July note, that the United States "would regard any subsequent sinkings as deliberately unfriendly." America was on the way to war.

There followed campaigns of minelaying off the east coast of Britain and in the English Channel by submarines of the German Navy, and significant U-boat activity in the Mediterranean through much of the remainder of the war.

In November 1915, an incident occurred in which the submarine U-38 sank the Italian steamer SS *Ancona,* which happened to be carrying forty American citizens. The *Ancona* had been sailing under an Austrian flag and the event caused the Germans to abandon their unrestricted submarine warfare policy. By January 1917, though, Germany's fortunes in the war were diminishing rapidly; the campaign in France was going badly, and the German Navy was essentially bottled up in its Kiel home port. The British blockade was causing a major food shortage in Germany and the Kaiser was being urged to end the war by whatever means possible. On 31 January he signed an order to authorize the resumption of unrestricted submarine warfare. And in

response President Wilson severed diplomatic relations with Germany and the U.S. Congress declared war on her.

The reversion proved initially successful for the Germans, while the British, Dutch, French and Scandinavians argued about the merits and disadvantages of running their merchant ships in convoys, but by May a transatlantic convoy system had been established and, accompanied by escorting warships, this led to a significant increase in U-boat losses.

In 1918, America was beginning to experience the attentions of several German submarines known as U-cruisers, in attacks that continued

The La Pallice bunker basin.

until the end of the war in November.

By mid-1918 losses in the U-boat fleet had reached unacceptable levels; morale among the members of the *Ubootwaffe* was extremely low and it was now evident that Germany could not win the war. One of the earliest conditions of the armistice established by the Allies was the surrender of all German submarines. On 24 October 1918 all of the U-boats were ordered to cease offensive operations and re-turn to their home ports; all seaworthy German submarines were to be turned over to the Allies and all subs in the building yards were to broken up. By the end of the war, the total of shipping gross tonnage sunk by the U-boats of the German Navy was 12,850,815. Nearly 5,000 merchant ships had been sunk by U-boats with the loss of 15,000 Allied sailor's lives.

In the German submarine force of WWI, a total of 351 U-boats sailed on operations. Of these, 178 were sunk in combat and an additional 39 were lost to other causes. 179 were surrendered to the Allies; some 5,000 U-boat crewmen were killed in action.

The Treaty of Versailles at the end of WWI not only required Germany to surrender all her U-boats; it forbade her to possess any in the future. When Adolf Hitler took power in Germany in 1933, however, he resumed the construction of a submarine fleet for

the German Navy.

With the coming of the Second World War and the territories seized by the Nazis during their *blitzkrieg* invasions of Norway and western France, they acquired several air and naval bases, the latter enabling them to operate with much easier access to the Allied convoys that were their targets.

In their extensive preparations for the Second World War, the Nazis devoted much consideration to requirements for servicing, maintaining, and repairing, as well as sheltering their submarines from air attack. They took advantage of the many improvements achieved since the First World War in aerial weapons technology and that of air weapons delivery systems, to create the design and construction of the new submarine bunker facilities, or pens, to be built for them by the Organisation Todt which was brought in to administer the labour of the great project.

The problems faced by the Todt force included the logistics of the sand, timber, cement, and aggregate supply . . . and the steel that had to be brought in from Germany. Of perhaps greater concern to Todt management, though, was labour. In France, the recruitment of workers and the access to raw materials was easy enough; not so easy though in Norway where the population was much more reluctant to help the Germans. Construction itself was generally more difficult in Norway too, where the siting of the U-bunkers was normally at the head of fiords, requir-

ing the foundations and footings to be hewn from solid granite, with further problems to be overcome from several meters of silt. Another consideration in organising the project work was that a large percentage of the workforce was forced labour; concentration camp inmates provided by the SS from facilities nearby.

The Todt foremen had to overcome the distruptions to their schedules and the hampering of the supply of raw materials caused by frequent Allied air raids. These attacks damaged or destroyed portions of the structures in work, wrecked machinery and terrified the workers. Everyone involved had to somehow cope with relatively new technology in the piledrivers, excavators, concrete pumps, cranes, and floodlighting, all of which could be

The huge torpedo store at La Pallice.

temperamental. The fundamental design aspects of the U-bunkers called for far more than just accommodation for the key occupants, the submarines. The pens had to provide the space and facilities for the many offices, accommodation for the more important personnel including crewmen, medical facilities, ventilators, lavatories, generators, communications, workshops, radio testing facilities, kitchens, and the water purification plants, as well as storage space for ammunition, spares, explosives and oil and the anti-aircraft gun positions.

If there is such a thing as a typical example of the development of a pen shelter complex on the Brittany coast of France, perhaps it would be that of St Nazaire. One of the largest ports on the French Atlantic coast before

the Second World War, St Nazaire was occupied by the German Army in June 1940 with submarine operations from it starting in September. By December the Todt Organisation personnel were looking into the feasibility of building a new U-boat base there that would be wholly protected from aerial bombing. The construction began in February 1941, with principal work continuing through June1942. A fortified lock was built in 1943-44 to protect U-boats as they transitted between the pens and the Loire River. The pens facility is 300 metres long, 130 metres wide and 18 metres high. There are 14 sub pens, each holding two boats and the base was equipped with 150 offices, four kitchens, a hospital, 92 dormitories for submarine crews, two electrical plants and 97 magazines.

Even the various special interest factions within the German Navy all concluded in the 1930s that in the next war a new and extraordinarily designed type of structure would be essential to shelter and protect the German submarine force from air attacks. Still, other military priorities took precidence and a lengthy delay ensued before work would begin on the massive U-bunker project of complexes that would appear along the Atlantic coast of France in Brittany. It was an early raid on Berlin by bombers of the Royal Air Force that motivated the German chancellor Adolf Hitler to order the construction of three huge anti-aircraft "flak towers" in the capital that ultimately led to development of the U-bunker construction project. The German leader had wanted peace with the British but his efforts in that direction failed and he then decided to develop some of the Brittany seaports that his forces were occupying and directed the Organisation Todt to proceed on a higher priority with planning for the first of the U-boat bunkers he was to create. These initial efforts would be built not in France but in Hamburg (Elbe II) and on the island of Heligoland (Nord-

A metallurgical repair facility within the Bordeaux U-bunker complex in the 1990s.

see III), with early work beginning in autumn 1940. In the building programme that followed, more than four million cubic meters of concrete were poured in the construction of the five primary U-bunker complexes in Brittany and the many related secondary facilities that were built in Germany, France and Norway. The German facilities included two structures in Hamburg (Elbe II and Fink II), the latter built mainly by slave labour in a four-year effort. Late in the war it was captured by the Allies and destroyed. A base was built at Danzig (now Gdansk in Poland) but it was lo-

cated out of range of enemy aircraft, and no submarine pens were built there. Other German pen complexes included two in Bremen (Valentin and Hornisse). Work on the latter began in 1944 but it was never completed. The Valentin bunker was the largest such facility in Germany and was intended for the manufacture of the Type XXI submarine but it too was not completed. American and British bomb types were tested there and it was used for a time as a storage facility by the German Navy. Valentin was built by labourers provided by the Neuengamme concentration camp.

Another site of U-bunker building was Kiel where two complexes, the Killian and Konrad bunkers, were constructed beginning in 1941 and 1942 respectively. Both were frequently bombed by the Allies during the war. The Konrad site was used in the construction of *Seehund* midget submarines. In a strange wartime incident, the submarine U-4708, was berthing in a pen at the Killian bunker when some off-target bombs falling near the town created a tsunami wave which swamped the U-boat. Some of its hatches were open and the boat sank in the pen despite being sheltered in the bunker. Heligoland was undamaged in the war years until 1945 when it was attacked by the RAF. Nothing remains of it today. Work on the Type XXI submarine was carried out in pen shelters for Blohm & Voss at Hamburg; for AG Weser at Bremen; and for F. Schichau at Danzig.

The most difficult and demanding construction site activity for the Todt workforces was in Norway where the severity of the weather for much of the time slowed their progress considerably. Siting near the ends of fiords brought footing and foundation problems leading to construction defects. Too, the fall of France to the Germans in June 1940 somewhat restricted the priority of the pen construction in Norway until the liberation of France after the Normandy invasion. Construction work at the Bruno pen facilities in Bergen was plagued by weather, a shortage of vital raw materials, local labour problems and a lack of specialized machinery, tools and equipment. Equally problematic was the worksite at Trondheim known as Dora I where work was begun in 1941 just after the German invasion of the Soviet Union. An ample supply of labour was provided there by Russian prisoners of war. But the difficulties created by the siting locations resulted in major trouble with the foundations.

In France, work on the St Nazaire U-boat base began in 1941. With the arrival of U-46, German submarine operations began from the St Nazaire port in late September 1940. Officials of the Todt group went to St Nazaire in December of that year to evaluate it as a site for a new submarine base capable of protecting and sheltering U-boats from British air attack. The site was approved for that purpose and construction of the new bunker complex was started in February 1941. By 1944, a fortified lock had been completed there to protect the U-boats in their brief journeys to and from the pens and the Loire River. St Nazaire was the location of Operation Chariot, the 1942 British commando raid in which a drydock adjacent to the pens was wrecked when an explosive-packed destroyer was rammed into it. The U-boat pens were not attacked in the raid.

It was the largest of the U-boat bases, the Keroman base at Lorient. It was comprised of the three main

Keroman bunkers, the Scorff bunker and the two Dom bunkers (Dom referring to their cathedral-like design), all of them under construction in 1941, with two further bunkers in the planning phase.

The Keroman I and II structures were served by an unusual, custom-built system in which their submarines were hauled from the water, positioned on a multi-wheeled buggy and moved into the bunker on a sliding bridge device. It was more vulnerable to air raid attack with the boat exposed on the bridge for a brief period, but it had the advantage of not requiring a drydock facility. In another unique inovation of the Lorient complex, the two Dom bunkers were positioned around a large turntable that received and delivered into covered repair bays. Added significance of the Lorient base was afforded by the presence of Grossadmiral Karl Dönitz, Commander of the U-boats, who made his headquarters at Kerneval, Lorient.

La Pallice and La Rochelle are only six kilometres apart in Brittany. Work on the great bunker at La Pallice was started in April 1941 and was hosting its first submarines only six months later. Many movie-goers will be familiar with the base as it was a location for some of the scenes in the 1981 film *Das Boot*.

Like some of the other U-bunkers in Brittany, La Pallice was built with a double roof, the lower part being made of 3.5 metres of reinforced concrete with the upper roof being made of concrete beams with one metre space between them.

Workers of the Todt organisation prepare armatures for concrete pen structures at the La Pallice U-bunker.

French Atlantic coast U-bunker facilities. The lone pen bunker there was built in a year and completed in 1942. Except for limited attention from U.S. Army Air Force bombers in 1943, the Brest base was mostly undamaged in the war, and the Germans garrisoned there surrendered the facility to the American forces in September 1944.

When the war began in 1939, the city of Bordeaux was the fourth largest in France. Construction of the massive U-bunker there was begun in 1941. The Bordeaux U-bunker port was the

The bunker was subjected to several air raid attacks in August 1944 and was hit by six of the massive Tallboy bombs which, while heavily damaging the upper roof, failed to penetrate the lower roof. No U-boats were damaged in the attack. In September, Allied forces surrounded the base and lay siege to it. But the La Pallice complex was being defended by some 20,000 German troops and was not surrendered until the end of the war. It is notable that all food, fuel and supplies in that period were delivered to the base by submarine. The final such delivery was made on 3 May 1945 by a Type VII U-boat and was followed on the 8th by the capitulation of the base to the Allies. In addition to *Das Boot*, other films have used the base as a shooting location, including *Indiana Jones II*. Today a portion of the bunker is used by the French Navy for storage.

The largest of all the U-bunkers was that of Brest, northernmost of the

left: Pre-fabricated accommodation buildings for the use of the 2nd U-Flotilla at Lorient; right: A machine-gun port at La Pallice; below: A French submarine of the 1990s at Lorient.

site of the British Operation Frankton, in which a commando unit, the Royal Marines Boom Patrol Detachment, carried out a raid on shipping in the French harbour of Bordeaux. The plan called for the small unit, together with six canoes, to be delivered by submarine to the Gironde Estuary from which they would paddle at night to Bordeaux. There they were to attack the docked vessels with Limpet mines and then escape to Spain. The unit was made up of twelve specially trained men including their commander, Her-

Repair work in the marina of Bordeaux U-bunker.

bert Hasler. From the start one of the canoes was damaged. It and its crew were unable to take part in the raid. In the end just two of the ten men who went on the raid survived: they were Hasler and Bill Sparks, his number two in their canoe. Of the remaining eight, six were captured and executed by the Germans. The other two died of hypothermia. The raid was based on the Bordeaux port being a prime destination for supplies in aid of the German war effort, including up to the date of the raid some 25,000 tons of crude rubber. The plan required the men to soemhow avoid contact with the more than thirty German Navy vessels then patrolling or using the big port. The aim of the commandoes

was to sink at least six of the cargo ships in the harbour.

The commando preparation for the raid required all of the men to become skilled in canoe handling, Limpet mine handling, submarine rehearsals and escape and evasion. Their canoes were given the code-name Cockle. They were semi-rigid two-man canoes with canvas sides and flat bottoms, fifteen feet long, fully collapsible and capable of being manhandled through the narrow confines of a submarine to the storage area where they would be erected and then hauled out of the hull via the submarine torpedo hatch. On the raid, each canoe would have to carry its two man crew, three sets of paddles, eight Limpet mines, a compass, a repair bag, a torch, a depth

below: The eastern Dombunker a cathedral-like repair structure at Lorient; right: An end-view of the U-bunker at Brest.

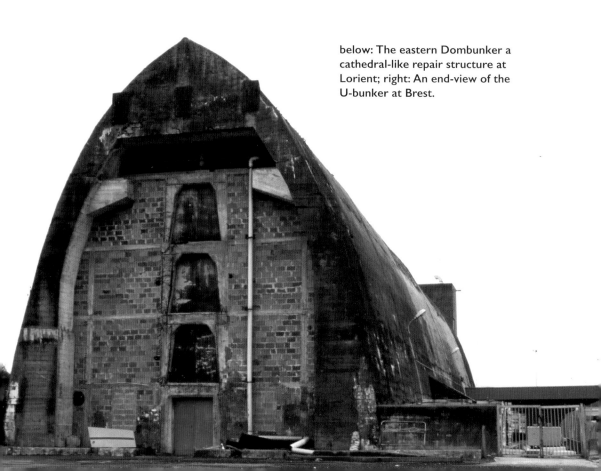

sounding reel, a camouflage net, a waterproof watch, a fishing line, two hand grenades, water and rations for six days, a spanner to activate the mines and a magnet to hold the canoe against the sides of the cargo ships. Each man also carried a .45 ACP pistol and a Fairbairn-Sykes fighting knife.

The Royal Navy submarine HMS *Tuna* left Holy Lock, Scotland with the raiders and their six canoes on aboard on 30 November 1942. The plan called for them to reach the Gironde Estuary on 6 December. The sub finally reached the estuary on the 7th and surfaced ten miles from its mouth. With a canoe damaged while being taken off the sub, the five remaining canoe crews left the sub at 1930. On their paddling journey toward the target,

they encountered strong winds and tides and soon one of the canoes disappeared. They later encountered five-foot waves and another of the canoes was lost when it capsized. The two crewmen managed to swim to shore. As the three remaining canoes approached a checkpoint in the river they came upon three German frigates, avoided them and covered 20 miles in the next five hours, landing at St Vivien du Medoc. By the end of the second night only two canoes remained and they had covered a further 22 miles. The various problems and hazards they encountered caused Hasler to change the plan for the attack and reset it for the night of 11/12 December. On the last day the two remaining crews made their Limpet mines ready and set them

below: Base buildings fitted with gun-ports at La Pallice; right: A built-over pen at Lorient.

to detonate at 2100. Before they had left on the raid, each of the canoes had been given a codename. The remaining canoes were *Catfish* and *Crayfish*, and Hasler decided that *Catfish* would cover the western side of the Bordeaux docks; *Crayfish* the eastern side.

The two surviving crews found their way to Bordeaux on 11/12 December, night five in calm clear weather. Starting at 2100, Hasler and Sparks in *Catfish* were able to place eight Limpet mines on ships in the western side of the dock.

By 0045 all their mines had been planted and they had left the harbour. Mills and Laver in *Crayfish* found no target vessels on the east side of the dock so they moved on to Bassens where they placed eight mines; five on a large cargo ship and the other three on a small liner. The two canoe crews met on their way down river and continued together until 0600 when they beached their canoes near St Genes de Blaye. The two crews then went off separately for the Spanish border. Two days later,

Laver and Mills were apprehended by the Gendarmerie and turned over to the Germans. Six days and 100 miles later, Hasler and Sparks finally arrived at the town of Ruffec where they contacted members of the French Resistance, who took them to a farm where they spent the next eighteen days in hiding before being guided through the Pyrenees into Spain. With more help from the French Resistance, Hasler made it back to Britain on 2 April and Sparks arrived there somewhat later.

In the aftermath of the raid, the Germans announced that sabotagers had been caught and killed near the mouth of the Gironde on 8 December, and later confirmed the damage by mysterious explosions to five ships in Bordeaux harbour. Many years later extensive damage to a sixth vessel was revealed through research. Further research showed that the other five damaged ships were, in fact, returned to service shortly after the raid.

Sheard and Moffatt had, in fact, not

Sailboats sheltering in the great
U-bunker at Bordeaux; right: A
drydock in use at Bordeaux.

drowned on the first night of the raid as believed, but had later succombed to hypothermia.

In 1955, a fictionalized version of the raid was made into a film that was called *The Cockleshell Heroes*. It was made by Warwick Films and starred Anthony Newly, Trevor Howard, David Lodge and José Ferrer and was directed by Ferrer.

In 2002, the Frankton Trail, a walking path tracing the 100-mile route of Hasler and Sparks on foot through occupied France, was estblished to perpetuate the history of the raid. Today, the waters of the Bordeaux U-bunker basin are calm; boat owners work on their vessels and civilian sailors tend to their sailboats in the former submarine pens.

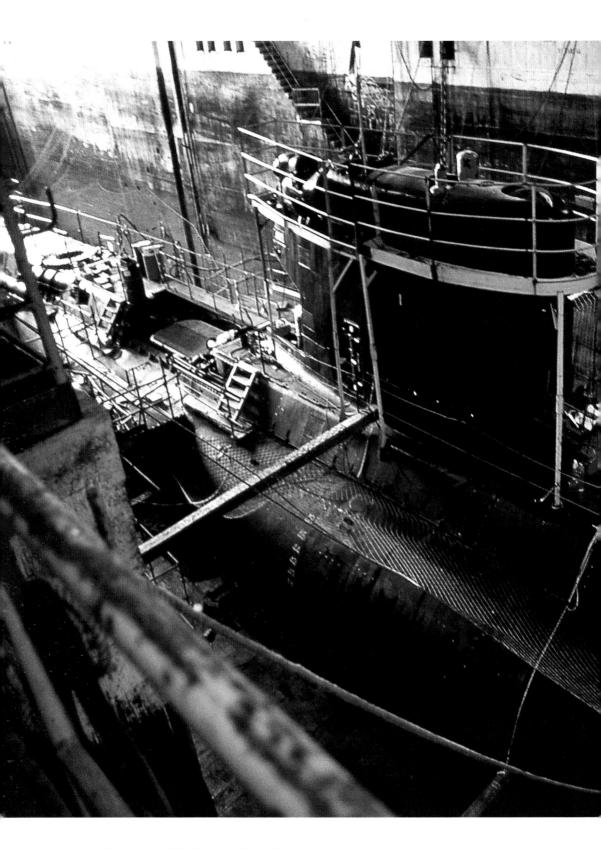

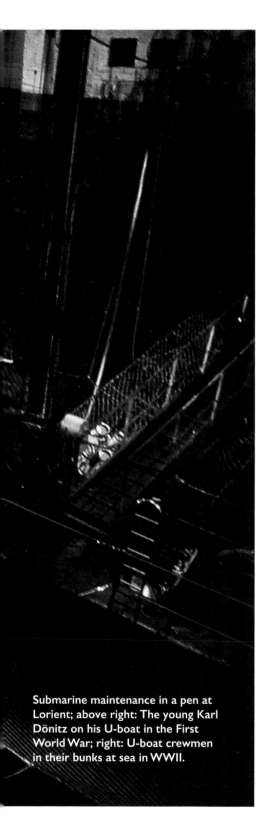

Submarine maintenance in a pen at
Lorient; above right: The young Karl
Dönitz on his U-boat in the First
World War; right: U-boat crewmen
in their bunks at sea in WWII.

They evolved from the U-boats of the First World War, the U-18 series of 1916. Of all the submarine designs built by German manufacturers over the years since that war, the Type VIIC ocean-going U-boat was by far the dominant type and the exemplar of submarines which the German Navy would take to war.

After the end of that war, and with the harsh and punitive terms of the Versailles Treaty as perceived by the Germans, they elected to remain connected to the submarine world through the design of a new sub, the Type VII, with the help of a dummy Dutch company, Ingenieurskantoor voor Scheepsbouw, Den Haag, an entity established by Germany after the war to develop and maintain submarine technology and circumvent the Versailles Treaty limitations. The product was built in various shipyards the world over. Other projects that influenced the design and construction of the VII were the Spanish E-1 boat, and the Finnish *Vetehinen* class boat. Together with the Type I, they helped provide the basis for the Type VII.

The Type VII was the most widely used U-boat in the Second World War and, with 703 examples built, the most produced submarine class in history. It was the submarine type most used in the Battle of the Atlantic. In that campaign, the Type VIIs were responsible for nearly 60 per cent of all the U-boat successes.

The VIIC, 221 feet from its shark-like bow to the narrow stern; it had a

THE TYPE VII

A preserved example of a Type VIIC U-boat on the beach at Laboe in northern Germany. The U-995 served in the Kriegsmarine from 1943 until the end of the war.

draught of 15 feet, a beam of 20 feet 6 inches, and a displacement of 769 tons. When properly handled it could be totally submerged in about twenty seconds from the order "Dive!"

Like other submarines of the time, these were not pure submarines in terms of their performance. They were submersibles . . . capable of diving to an authorized safe diving depth of 330 feet, not all that much deeper than their own length—compared to a modern American *Los Angeles* 688 Class nuclear attack sub, with a length of 362 feet and a listed test depth of 800 feet (though this author has been to a depth of 1,000 feet in the USS *Jefferson City* 688 Class, and *Jane's Fighting Ships 2004-2005 Edition*, lists its maximum dive depth as 1,475 feet), redefining true submarine. The original Type VII–

the A model–was designed in 1933 as the first of a new series of Type VII boats, most of which were constructed at AG Weser, Bremen. Though the most narrow, cramped and confining of the VII series boats, the As were popular with their crewmen because they could crash-dive faster than bigger and slower submarines, making them safer and providing more protection, at least in the perception of their crews. They also liked the relatively shorter endurance of the smaller boat which made their patrols briefer. In performance, the VII was more powerful than the Type II it replaced and it was well armed with four bow torpedo tubes and one stern tube. It carried up to eleven torpedoes on board and, when operating on the surface, the VII was relatively agile. It was also armed with

left: Torpedomen, or "mixers" at work in wartime; right: A U-boat returning to its Brittany base.

a 3.5-inch deck gun and 220 rounds of ammunition. On the surface, the VIIA was powered by two MAN AG six-cylinder M6V diesel engines generating a total of up to 2,310 brake horsepower. When travelling submerged it was pro-pelled by two Brown, Boveri & Cie double-acting electric motors giving a total of 750 horsepower.

"You are now a prize of the German Navy. You will set course for Bordeaux and on arrival inform the port authorities you have been captured by U-99 and sent there to be taken as prize. Do you understand? Do not try to get away be-cause I shall be following you below the surface. One deviation from your course and I shall torpedo you. Do you understand that?"—Otto Kretschmer to the captain of an Estonian freighter

The real workhorse U-boat of the Atlantic battle was the Type VIIC, of which 568 were commissioned between 1940 and 1945. The Type VIIC came into service near the start of the war and was still in service when the anti-sub efforts of the Allies ended the campaign of the U-boats in 1944.

Unlike its predecessors, the VIIC had an active sonar system and a few other improvements. These made it a few feet longer and eight tons heavier. Later in the war many Type VIIs were fitted with snorkels; devices which enabled a sub-marine to operate submerged while taking in air from the surface. The British called it the "Snort" and it was actually a Dutch development that was widely used on German U-boats in the latter part of WWII.

Until the introduction of the nuclear-powered submarine in the 1950s, subs were basically designed to operate mainly on the surface, submerging for daylight attacks and evasion. In the early 1940s, U-boats and other submarines operating by night were safer on the surface because, while sonar could readily detect boats underwater, it was nearly useless against a surface vessel. But, as radar was improved in the course of the war, the U-boats were forced to operate more and more underwater, running on their electric motors with greatly limited speed and range. By 1943 so many U-boats were being lost in action that many of the remaining Type VIIs and Type IXs were retrofitted with snorkels and by early 1944 were using snorkels

operationally with roughly half the boats based in the French U-bunkers having them fitted.

Operationally, the U-boat crews soon discovered problems in operation with the snorkel equipment. With the snorkel raised in the operating position, the U-boat was limited to a six-knot speed to avoid breaking the snorkel tube and with the diesel engines running in that condition the sound-detection equipment of the submarine was all but useless. Most threatening was the fact that the snorkels were equipped with automatic valves to prevent seawater being sucked into the diesel engines under water. When these valves slammed shut the engines would draw

A rare colour image of an original U-boat captain's cap. This one is displayed at the U-Boot Archiv in Altenbruch, Germany.

air from the boat itself before shutting down, causing a partial vacuum and extreme pain to the ears of the crew members, sometimes even rupturing eardrums, a problem that still exists in some later model diesel submarines and even in some nuclear subs. It has largely been eliminated, however, by the use of high-vacuum cut-off sensors that shut down the engines when a vacuum in the boat reaches a pre-set level. There are aspects of the snorkel operation that detract from what it offers. When operating submerged on snorkel in clear weather, the exhaust from the diesels can be seen on the sur-face to a distance of up to three miles.

In comparison with the Type VII, the

Type IXC was somewhat heavier at 1,120 tons, a bit wider in the beam and thirty feet longer. With a broader deck and bigger conning tower it took up to ten seconds longer to submerge than the Type VII, depending on conditions of the sea. Depth-wise, both types of boats could go up to twice as deep as the official safety limits and often did so when trying to survive depth-charge attacks.

On the surface, the VIIC's top speed was slightly under eighteen knots—a bit slower than the IX. Neither were as fast as a destroyer or a frigate, but were fast enough to outrun a corvette or sloop which they often encountered on convoy patrols.

When operating underwater and carrying a hundred tons of water bal-last to dampen its built-in buoyancy, the top speed was a mere 7.6 knots, which was just about fast enough to keep up with the faster convoys and overtake the slower ones.

The VIIC had a range of 9,700 nauti-cal miles, half that if the top speed was sustained. When underwater, running on the batteries at two knots, the range was about 180 nautical miles, reducing to 80 if the speed was four knots. But with a normal fuel load of 113.5 tons of heavy diesel oil, and the two MAN six-cylinder 1,400 hp engines cruising at a speed of ten knots, the VIIC could generally achieve that 9,700-mile range.

The Type IX, on the other hand, had an 11,000 nautical mile range when sailing at its best speed; 16,000 at an economical speed and just 134 when running at four knots submerged.

While the VIIC was equipped with four torpedo tubes in the bow and one in the stern, the IXC had four in the bow and two in the stern. The VIIC carried between eleven and fourteen torpedoes, depending on the particular assignment and the range of the patrol, the IX could carry up to twenty-two. The deck armament varied, but the standard ordnance consisted of an 88mm gun forward of the conning tower, with a 37mm gun and two 20mm machine-guns mounted on a platform which the Germans called a wintergarden and the British referred to as a bandstand, abaft the bridge. All together it provided weaponry that was more than adequate for shooting up a merchant ship or defending against a low-flying aircraft, but not perhaps sufficient for a gunfight with a corvette or a sloop, and certainly not with a destroyer.

For the most part, the Type VIICs were strictly employed on offensive patrols and their hunting grounds stretched from the North Atlantic to the Baltic and from the Mediterranean to the Arctic. Type IXs could and did range as far as the South Atlantic, the west coast of Africa, and the Caribbean. The Type IX offered some versatility. In addition to performing as a combat weapon, she could be used as a supply vessel carrying fuel, ammunition, and provisions for other combat U-boats at sea. These were called "milch cows". Theoretically, they could keep the VIICs on station

for as long as there was a convoy to attack or until Admiral Dönitz called them back to their bases in Brittany. In another comparison with the Type VII, the longer hull of the IX meant for the crew a slightly less cramped environment than in the VII, which really mattered to the crews as they could expect to be at sea for up to fourteen weeks as compared with the five or six weeks of a typical Type VII patrol.

The stern torpedo room of the IX was more spacious than that of the VII and afforded more bunk space for the crewmen, and a man could slightly more easily sit down in the lavatory, though his knees would still be up against the wall. In practical terms, though, there was little real difference below decks between the VII and the IX. Not a single cubic inch of space was wasted within the hull of either boat. Tables all folded up; foodstuffs hung everywhere; The back of every seat was a locker and every mess room bench doubled as a bed.

The control room was amidships, with the conning tower above; the fuel and main water ballast tanks below. The control room was twenty-two feet long and twenty feet across. It was absolutely crammed with levers for the ballast tanks, buttons and spin wheels that worked the hydroplanes and vents, the Papenberg depth gauge, the Zeiss attack periscope, the navigator's table, the gyro and magnetic compasses and the electric steering gear. It was the nerve centre of the boat and the conning tower was its fighting heart. The conning tower con-

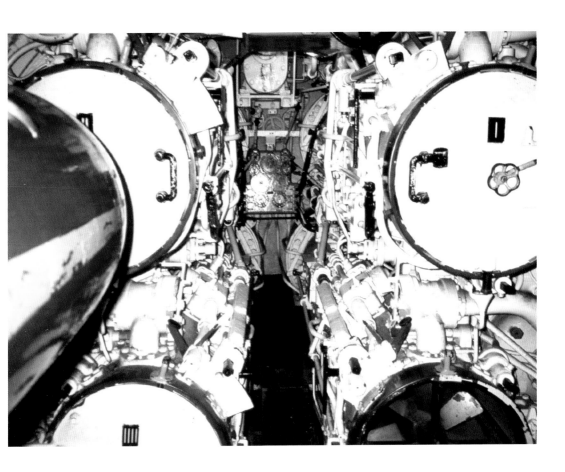

top: The forward torpedo room of U-995, a Type VII boat; above: Construction of a U-boat hull.

left and right: At sea aboard a Type VII boat in WWII.

tained the helm and the navigation or sky periscope, the Siemans-Schukert torpedo computer linked to the bridge master sight and the gyro compass, as well as the fire interval calculator. The helmsman steered the boat from the tower or the control room, turning the rudders by the pressure of a button, or in emergency, by a hand steering system aft in the electric motor room. He always steered the vessel 'blind', changing and maintaining course by the compass, like a pilot flying in cloud.

The control room was separated by dished watertight bulkheads from the fore and aft sections of the boat. Moving forward a crewman would pass between the radio and sound rooms to starboard and the cubicle that served as the commander's cabin to port. After this he would pass through the officers' wardroom and quarters, past the twin lavatories (one of which doubled as a supplementary food store for the first weeks of the patrol), and through the petty officer's mess into the bow compartment—the 'bug room'. Tiers of narrow cots on both sides of the boat, with hammocks slung between, provided the crew quarters, and they took their meals at a central folding table. The crewmen shared the compartment with the reserve torpedoes, which were chained above their bunks.

Moving aft of the control room, the prowling seaman would pass in turn through a combined utility room and petty officers' quarters, the galley, past the bulk of the one-ton air compres-

sor, into the electric motor room and stern torpedo storage, and through the diesel engine room to reach the stern tube.

The normal ship's company in a Type VIIC was forty-four: four commissioned officers—the Commander, with the 1st and 2nd Officers and the Chief Engineer—and ten Petty Officers responsible for the watches, the engine rooms, the electrics, the radio and control rooms, with a quarter-

Günther Prien commanded the U-boat that sank the British battleship *Royal Oak* at Scapa Flow in October 1939.

crew usually included a sailor with some first-aid experience. The larger boats normally carried a qualified doctor, seconded for duty with the U-boat arm. For sea emergencies the crews were equipped with inflatable life jackets, masks and breathing tubes and a twenty-man life raft was carried in the outer hull forward of the bridge.

Warning of an enemy radar being beamed towards a U-boat was dealt with in 1942 by a rather crude item of equipment, surprisingly so in view of all the other more sophisticated gadgetry on board. It was an item that any British sailor would have thought of as a "lash-up" It consisted of a bulky wooden frame shaped like a cross and and containing a wire antenna that could pick up radar transmission pulses at a range of up to twenty miles. The frame was mounted on the deck abaft the bridge. It was manually rotated by the telegraphist on watch and who, if he was able to distinguish the pulses through the whistling and cracking sounds in his headphones, could read off the bearing of the searching enemy ship or aircraft putting out the pulse. One difficulty with the "Biscay Cross" as it became known, was that when the boat submerged, the whole apparatus had to be taken inboard through the conning tower. In a crash-dive it was liable to be trampled under foot by the watch as they came down the ladder in a rush.

master, a coxswain, and a total of thirty seamen and technicians, including torpedo men, engine room artificers, electricians, telegraphists, control room hands, and a cook. Cramped as they were, the crew sometimes had to find room for passengers—official observers, newly-trained officers gaining combat experience, and the war correspondents—some of whom might be expected to pull their weight and take their share of the duties, while others only came aboard to get a glory story for the Propaganda Ministry.

The standard compliment of the Type IXC was ten officers and forty-four seamen, and while the Type VIIC's

In the summer of 1942, the Biscay Cross was superceded by "Metox", a legacy to Karl Dönitz from the fall of

France. It received signals in the short wave bands and was less of an encumbrance. Metox, though, became suspect when U-boats equipped with it were frequently attacked by Allied aircraft, which seemed to indicate that it acted like a homing device. That suspicion was compounded by the interrogation of a captured British pilot who said: "We don't need radar to find you chaps; we can pick you up on radio," the crafty airman lied.

The increasing number of attacks were due to the Allies latest centimetric radar, but the suspicion lingered on, and was enough to persuade Dönitz, when he was appraised of it, to order all U-boats at sea to switch it off. It did little for the morale of the boat crews to learn, albeit incorrectly, that they had been beaming their position to the enemy for the last five months.

From 1943, many Type IX U-boats were equipped with the snorkel and with a new radar detector replacing Metox. It was designated W.AnzG1 and nicknamed Wanze or Bedbug. It had Radio direction-finding (RDF) antennae, which was tactically useful but tended to extend the IX's dive time even further, and Aphrodite, a towed hydrogen balloon filled with strips of aluminium "Chaff:, like the Allied bomber's version "Window" intended to baffle the search radars.

Bedbug had automatic search control, which eliminated the need for manual rotation, but the telegraphist had to be quick to recognize a signal and hold the antenna on the bearing; furthermore, neither it nor its later versions entirely fitted the bill. The German Navy scientists still firmly believed that radar emissions in wave bands shorter than twenty centimetres would never give a good response, and they were only forced to reconsider early in 1943, when pieces salvaged from a downed RAF bomber revealed that a radar on a wave band below ten centimetres was in common use. Göring then demanded an all-out effort from his electronics experts to provide his night-fighters with a suitable detector, and in due course they came up with "Naxos", which was effective in the short wave bands, if only at close range. Naxos, however, came along too late for the U-boats. The German submarine arm had fallen behind in the electronics battle and, by the time Naxos was installed, there were so many Allied aircraft in the skies that life for the U-boat sailors had. become one long series of alarm dives.

"A life of action and danger moderates the dread of death. It not only gives us fortitude to bear pain, but teaches us at every step the precarious tenure on which we hold our present being.
—from *On The Fear of Death* by William Hazlitt

"The feeble tremble before opinion; the foolish defy it; the wise judge it; the skillful direct it."
—Mme Jeanne Roland

The pens of the
Bordeaux U-bunker.

If an injury has to be done to
a man it should be so severe
that his vengeance need not
be feared.
—from *The Prince*
by Niccolo Machiavelli

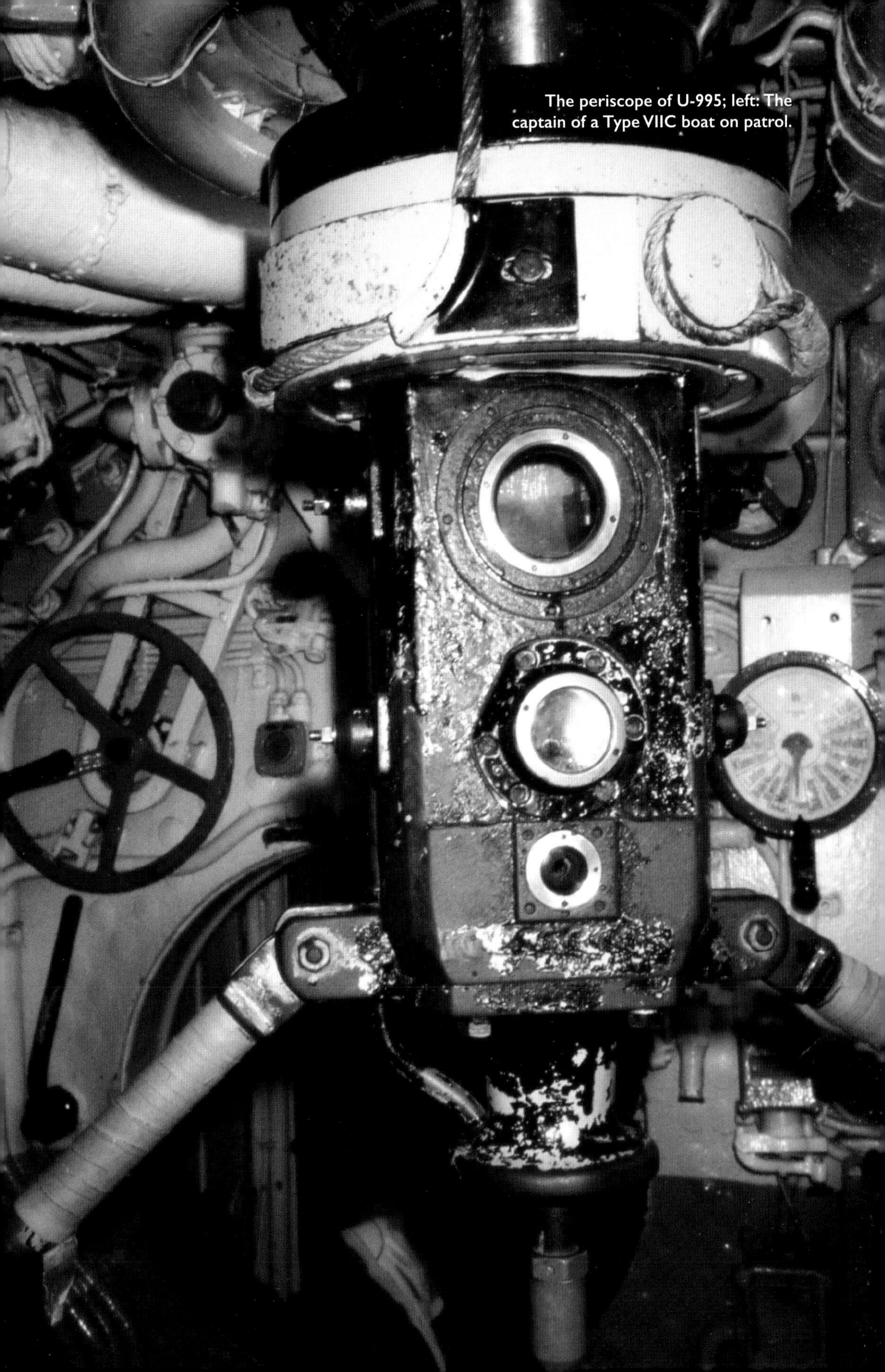
The periscope of U-995; left: The captain of a Type VIIC boat on patrol.

Submarine crew
survival testing

It grew quickly, the construction group known to the German government as the Organisation Todt, from a workforce of about 250,000 people in 1938 to more than 1.4 million by late in 1944. This was the group whose builders were called upon to create and construct the great U-boat bunker shelters along the French Atlantic coast and in Norway in the war years of the 1940s. But over the years since WWII, it has often been misinterpreted and its ef-

BRITTANY BASES

forts incorrectly explained. A civil engineer in the 1930s, Dr Fritz Todt was building roads in Germany in 1938 when Adolf Hitler asked him to plan and build what the British referred to as the Siegfried Line and the Germans called the West Wall. Not an actual wall, but a system of gun emplacements and anti-tank obstacles established along the western border of Germany. It was, in fact, a line of defensive fortresses and tank defences built east of the original Hindenburg

Line of WWI during the 1930s and stretching 390 miles. It featured more than 18,000 bunkers, many connecting tunnels and thousands of tank traps. Planning for the Line began in 1936 with construction mostly completed by 1940. From September 1944 until March 1945, an offensive at the Siegfried Line cost the Americans nearly 140,000 troops. German losses were not well documented.

Prior to that campaign, German propaganda frequently referred to the Siegfried Line as "an unbreach-able bulwark." The Line was the subject of a British popular song of the war years: We're going to hang out the washing on the Siegfried Line. / Have you any dirty washing, mother dear? / We're gonna hang out the washing on the Siegfried Line / 'Cause the washing day is here. / Whether the weather may be wet or fine / We'll just rub along without a care. / We're going to hang out the washing on the Siegfried Line If the Siegfried Line's still there . . . —(Kennedy/Carr) Peter Maurice Music Co Ltd 1939

The logistics of the enormous growth the Todt group went through in the war years required substantial recruitment, clothing, feeding and accommodating the huge workforce, transporting them to the worksites where they were needed, and constantly providing them the incentives needed to retain them, especially in connection with a project as gigantic and demanding as the construction of the Brittany U-boat bunkers.

In his book, *Hitler's U-Boat Bases*, Jak P. Mallman Showell states: "The U-boat bunkers are among the most complicated structures ever built, erected exceedingly fast under the most difficult circumstances. The colossal undertaking required more skill and effort than an underfed, conscripted workforce could provide and the majority of labourers were volunteers who were offered considerable incentives in the form of additional

The house used by Grossadmiral Karl Dönitz as his headquarters in Kerneval, Lorient during the Second World War.

pay and extra food rations to get the job done." He points out that "The construction of the U-boat bunkers was . . . a highly complicated, mechanized production process which relied upon skilled and co-ordinated teamwork from a large number of specialist firms. There were ample opportunities for sabotage to slow down the process or even bring the machinery grinding to a standstill, yet this rarely happened." Showell continues: "This international workforce, with no natural allegiance to Germany, was made up from many different cultures: North African Arabs, as well as men from virtually every European country were represented. Many of these people had lost their jobs to the war and were keen to have an opportunity of earning a living from German construction projects."

While initiating many of the major projects of Organisation Todt, Fritz Todt would not be able to follow most of them to completion. He was killed in a plane crash in February 1942 and was replaced in his position by the German architect and Reich Minister of Armaments and War Production for Nazi Germany, Albert Speer.

Within the range of military benefits accruing to the Nazis in June 1940 from the defeat of France and the capitualtion of the Low Countries was the acquisition of several air and sea bases in western Europe. The ports which then became available to Admiral Dönitz on the French Atlantic coast, from Brest in the north to Bordeaux in the south, reduced the distance the U-boats had to travel to their killing grounds in the Atlantic by many hundreds of miles, enabling them to stay on station for ten days longer than when they were based in German ports. They also forced merchant shipping bound for Britain from the east to eschew the south coast docks at Portsmouth, Plymouth and Southampton and take the long route round, by the Bristol and St George's Channels to the northwestern ports of Liverpool and Glasgow.

Dönitz was aware that the berths for his U-boats had to be protected from the raids of the Royal Air Force and he persuaded Hitler of the need. He was referred to the Minister of Construction—Dr Fritz Todt—who immediately put his workforce to the task. Organisation Todt, with German engineers and construction experts, and with the assistance of volunteer and conscripted French technicians and labourers, began construction at a small fishing port near Lorient, which had initially been thought of only as a staging post—somewhere to rearm, refuel and resupply U-boats—while the flotilla headquarters and administration remained back in Germany. But by the time the OT finished, Lorient was fully operational, with nineteen pens connected by channels to the harbour, massively protected and complete with all the necessary facilities—main services, fuel stores, the dry docks, workshops

A U-boat drydock at the
St Nazaire naval base on the
Brittany coast.

and accommodation, and defended by batteries of anti-aircraft guns. Known to the U-boat arm as "the ace of bases", Lorient was home to the 2nd and 10th Flotillas, each with twenty-five U-boats, most of them the Type IXC long-range vessel.

As the OT construction gangs steadily worked their way along the coast, building bunkers as they went, their progress was followed by incoming Type VIIC flotillas, also nominally twenty-five boats strong. The 3rd Flotilla moved into La Pallice, and later the 1st and 9th were based at Brest, and the 6th and 7th at Saint-Nazaire. Bordeaux housed the 12th Flotilla, with a miscellany of supply boats, mine-layers and refuellers, and a flotilla of some twenty-three sub-

marines from the Italian Navy. Everywhere, the massive concrete structures dwarfed all other buildings in the harbours. Aircraft flying above them seldom saw a U-boat—only the flat, camouflaged roofs of the pens where they were hidden while being serviced, reprovisioned or repaired.

It was while the bunkers were still being built that the RAF's bombers should have struck, but at the crucial moment, and despite Churchill's statement in the House of Commons that "from being a powerful ally, France has been converted into an enemy", the Chiefs of Staff were persuaded by the Foreign Office that in all humanity the bombers could not strike the land

and people of defeated France. Although many Frenchment embraced
the posture of the craven Vichy government, the majority of them did not,
and no attacks were mounted until it
was too late.

At last, as they had to be, London's
qualms were put aside, and the Brittany bases—Brest, Lorient, and Saint-
Nazaire came under air attack in
1942 and 1943. The results were dis-
appointing. The RAF heavy bombers,
committed to night attacks by their
flimsy armament and to saturation
bombing by their imperfect bombsights, effectively laid waste to a large
amount. of property in Lorient and
Saint-Nazaire, but seldom hit the
bunkers, and, when they did, they
barely scratched their surfaces, The

Fortresses and Liberators of the
U.S. Eighth Army Air Force based in
Britain bombed with more precision,
but their 2,000-pounders merely
bounced off the concrete roofs and
walls: the bombs then available to
the RAF and the USAAF were not
designed to penetrate the fifteen or
twenty feet of reinforced concrete
of which the bunkers were constructed.

Brest, Lorient and Bordeaux were
natural harbours, whereas Saint-
Nazaire and La Pallice were not—
they needed lock gates to keep the
water level constant—but even
these were not attacked until the
summer of 1943, when the Eighth
Air Force made just one attack on
each. Bordeaux was never seriously

attacked at all. As for the bunkers, it was not until 1944, when the RAF combined three 4,000-pound "cookies" into a single armour-piercing "Tallboy" bomb, that they could be hurt at all.

Of his command's attacks in early 1943, Air Chief Marshal Arthur Harris wrote: "The most we could hope to do was to cause universal devastation round the [sub] pens and in the town. We could also give U-boat crews on shore a disturbed night. If they were foolish enough to stay in the area, but of course they were not. The Admiralty may or may not have thought that this would exert a worthwhile influence on the Battle of the Atlantic . . . though before we began on it I protested repeatedly against this hopeless misuse of air power. The only effect [the attacks] had was to delay the opening of the Battle of the Ruhr and the main bomber offensive against Germany by nearly two months."

The Biscay bases were well-defended by Luftwaffe fighters and by 88mm anti-aircraft guns, and in the course of the attacks more than a hundred aircraft were shot down, over half of them USAAF bombers. Like Air Chief Marshal Harris, General Spaatz had doubts about the policy, and in October 1942 he wrote to General Arnold, his C-in-C in Washington: "Whether or not these operations will prove too costly for the results obtained remains to be seen. The concrete submarine pens are hard, maybe impossible nuts to crack." Accepting, however, "that the bombing of the surrounding instal-lations should seriously handicap the effective use of the bases", he sent the bombers of the Eighth Air Force on eleven missions to the Brittany bases between October 1942 and April 1943, when both he and Air Chief Marshal Harris were given new priorities.

A French woman who had been a girl of five at the time, would always remember vividly the shooting down of one particular bomber. "Our house in Brest was destroyed", she said, "but a few days earlier we had fled to a remote village. I was told that the 'Brestois' in their shelters prayed for the RAF pilots while the bombs were falling. On 13th August 1943, an aircraft fell in a field near our village. At the funeral of the crew, German soldiers forbade the locals to enter the church. The silence of what seemed to me a vast crowd was very impressive. When the procession came out, the crowd moved forward but was stopped at the gate of the cemetery. I broke through the row of soldiers and followed the procession. A German officer looked down at me but didn't say anything. Always, when we passed the cemetery we prayed for the British pilots, and when spring came we brought bouquets of primroses."

Meanwhile, more than 600 Frenchmen were killed by the bombers, and their deaths were regretted in London and Washington. Patriotic French men and women, however, members of the Resistance and the Maquis, shed few tears over those of their countrymen who died while willingly working for the Germans in the harbours. By

ATELIERS METALLURGIQUES
DE LA BASE
Fabrication · Réparation · TP
tel: 56·50·85·88

ENTRÉE INTERDITE AUX
VOITURES DE TOURISME

GCA

A metallurgical repair facility at the
Bordeaux bunker in the 1990s.

U-boat crewmen; right:
right: A boat slipway at
the Lorient base.

mid-1943, the streets of Saint-Nazaire and Lorient were full of rubble, trade and traffic were halted and dwelling houses were ruined; the deep-sea fishing boats were moored and beached, because the fishermen either had no fuel or were afraid to put out on the mine-infested waters; all the schools were closed and the children were sent away into the country. Like them, the U-boat crews (as Arthur Harris had perceived) were moved well out of town for their R and R between patrols.

When the 'Happy Time' was over and Allied aircraft swept the skies of Europe and covered the approaches to the French Atlantic coast, the passage of the U-boats to and from their bases was always fraught with danger.

They were constantly obliged to dive to escape attack, and they were guided by trawlers or patrol boats into harbour through the mine-fields, which were regularly reseeded. They came in with decks awash and flooded ballast tanks, ready for a crash-dive at the first alarm; sometimes in shallow water, they stopped engines and hid among the inshore sardine boats until the RAF had gone. It was only when they reached the shelter of the pens that they were safe.

There, the scene was more reassuring, still giving the impression of German industry and strength. A sleek row of U-boats lay in water like a millpond, contrasting strangely with the shattered buildings of the harbour town; other boats were propped up in dry dock, while local harbour gangs were working on the hulls. As the crewmen came ashore, the sound of organized activity was everywhere, and the familiar, mingled smells of sea salt, oil and paint, the walls towered around them, dripping condensation and coldly reflecting the flames of welding burners; they passed ranks of cranes and derricks, great retorts of acid for the batteries, busy teams of workers and uniformed officials who saluted their Commander. They could easily have been in Hamburg, Kiel or Wilhelmshaven.

This, however, was defeated France, apparently complacent yet potentially hostile and subversive. Most of the above-water repair work was being carried out by French technicians, and whenever some inexplicable defect in the boat revealed itself at sea, suspicions of sabotage arose—suspicions that were always impossible to prove.

"Despite the most rigid checks by the Gestapo on the French shipyard work-ers, underground agents acutally wormed their way into the yards where the U-boats were readied for their next cruises. These seeming col-laborators, ostensibly working for the Germans, slipped little bags of sugar into the lubricating oil tanks of U-boats. The sugar dissolved into the oil and those U-boats came limping back to Lorient with their engines in sad shape. The underground agents made sound-looking welds on pres-sure fittings that would give way when the boat went deep.Some

skippers who didn't take their boats down to maximum depth on trial runs, are on the bottom of the ocean now with their whole crews because these welds gave way under attack. Workmen drilled small holes in the tops of fuel tanks and plugged the holes with stuff that was soluble in salt water. A few days after this boat went to sea, the plug would dissolve and the boat would leave a tell-tale oil streak behind her when she submerged.

"It was impossible to keep secrets in a base such as Lorient. The whole life of the town revolved around the operations of the U-boat fleet and everyone in town rubbed elbows with the U-boats one way or another. The shipyard workers, of course, got right

down inside them. Tradesmen delivered food to the boats, and any fool could tell from their grocery orders when a boat was about to sail. A brass band met boats returning from a successful patrol and the boats came up the river proudly displaying pennants with the names of their victims printed on them for anyone to see. Bartenders, waitresses, and gals of the evening took intimate parts in the continual round of arrival and departure binges. Anyone who kept his ears open after the first five or six rounds of drinks, could pick up many items of secret official information."
—from *Twenty Million Tons Under The Sea*
by Rear Admiral Daniel V. Gallery,

"It was not until the end of 1943 that USAAF surveys of strategic bombing results tended to confirm doubts hitherto hesitantly expressed regarding the value of bombing submarine bases. By that time the submarine had been defeated in the first round of the battle of supply, and it had become apparent that attack from the air against the U-boat at sea had been the most effecive single factor in reducing the German submarine fleet, and that bombing of bases had contributed relatively little in that direction. Grand Admiral Karl Dönitz, who as one-time commander of the U-boat fleet, was in a unique position to know whereof he spoke, later confirmed

this opinion in an interview with Allied intelligence officers after his capture in 1945. Not only were the pens themselves impervious to anything but the heaviest type of bomb, he asserted, but they housed virtually all necessary repair and maintenance facilities. Bombing of surrounding installations did not therefore seriously affect the rate of turn-around. What slowed turn-around most effectively, he claimed, was the necessity for repairing the damage done to hull structures by aerial bomb and depth-charge attacks delivered at sea."

—from *The Army Air Forces in World War II*
by Wesley F. Craven and James L.

"Looking back over this first phase of the effort against the U-boat bases, leaders chiefly concerned with its prosecution could come to few conclusions regarding its effectiveness; it was easy enough to compile and quote certain operational data; ground reports and aerial reconnaissance pointed to certain specific effects. But it was much more difficult to determine whether any significant number of months of U-boat operations had been denied the enemy through these operations or to what extent, if any, the American bombing attacks had affected the number of U-boats operating in the Atlantic. Information gained since the cessa-

left The art deco look of a building on the Lorient naval base complex; right: The second Dombunker at Lorient.

The St Nazaire bunker.

tion of hostilities indicates that the U-boats active in the Atlantic were steadily increasing in number during the period in question."
—from *The Army Air Forces in World War II*
by Wesley F. Craven and James L. Cate

"It was April 4, 1944, when the train deposited me in the ancient, charming, but somewhat delapidated town of Brest. An old bus took me through town, crossed the draw-bridge over the canal, coughed up-hill and continued westward on the familiar approach to the 1st U-boat Flotilla. I noticed a number of blimps floating gently over the harbour in the early

morning breeze. They were a new defense measure installed to protect the U-boat bunker from low-level air attacks.
—from *Iron Coffins*
by Herbert A. Werner

"If one U-boat skipper was consistently more successful than others under similar conditions, the staff would study his methods to see how he differed from the rest. It usually turned out that the big factor in outstanding success was the personality of the skipper, and the staff couldn't do much about that."
—from *Twenty Million Tons Under The Sea*
by Rear Admiral Daniel V; Gallery, USN

Throughout the most successful years of the Ubootwaffe, German newsreels, newspapers and journals regularly pictured U-boat commanders returning from the high seas, bearded, dressed in overalls, pea jackets and sea boots, and with the white-covered caps only they were authorized to wear, while fluttering on a wire behind them, victory pennants showed how many Allied vessels they had sunk on patrol. Photographs showed them gravely standing at attention to shake the admiral's hand, or, surrounded by their smiling crewmen, accepting the flowers, wine and kisses, and the plaudits of the crowd. Many U-boat commanders were *Oberleutnants*, a few were *Fregattenkapitäns* or higher, but the vast majority held the rank of *Kapitänleutnant*: "Herr Kaleu" to their crewmen, heroes to their admiral and to the German people.

One of Karl Dönitz's first actions when Gross Admiral Erich Raeder put him in charge of the U-boat force in 1936 was to turn the so-called Anti-Submarine School in Kiel into a training establishment for future U-boat officers. Three of

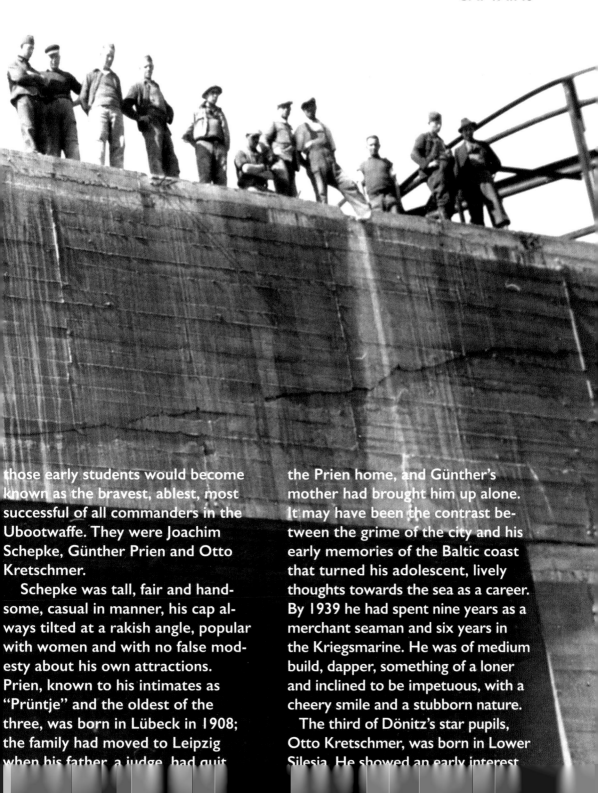

those early students would become known as the bravest, ablest, most successful of all commanders in the Ubootwaffe. They were Joachim Schepke, Günther Prien and Otto Kretschmer.

Schepke was tall, fair and handsome, casual in manner, his cap always tilted at a rakish angle, popular with women and with no false modesty about his own attractions. Prien, known to his intimates as "Prüntje" and the oldest of the three, was born in Lübeck in 1908; the family had moved to Leipzig when his father, a judge, had quit

the Prien home, and Günther's mother had brought him up alone. It may have been the contrast between the grime of the city and his early memories of the Baltic coast that turned his adolescent, lively thoughts towards the sea as a career. By 1939 he had spent nine years as a merchant seaman and six years in the Kriegsmarine. He was of medium build, dapper, something of a loner and inclined to be impetuous, with a cheery smile and a stubborn nature.

The third of Dönitz's star pupils, Otto Kretschmer, was born in Lower Silesia. He showed an early interest

German submarines back from patrol to the safety of their Brittany shelters.

in languages and science and was sent to study these subjects in England, France and Italy before enlisting as a naval cadet in 1930. Although, when World War II began, he welcomed the excitement of taking his "canoe", the 250-ton U-23, on early probing missions into the northern British waters—these missions came to be known as "Kretschmer's Shetland Sorties"—he shared the view of many of his colleagues that the full weight of the Wehrmacht should have been directed to the East. "Silent Otto" as he came to be known was hawk-nosed and slim, and an inveterate cigar smoker. He was intolerant of frailty but had a pleasant sense of fun. A mess-mate described him as a "friend of no one, popular with all". Probably, of the three future aces, Kretschmer had the keenest intellect and the strongest character.

In April 1940, Dönitz ordered Kretschmer to commission and command a new ocean-going Type VIIC, U-99, and this was the vessel in which he was to range the North Atlantic with deadly effect for the best part of a year. It was the fashion in the U-boat arm for the crew to paint their own insignia on the conning tower, a fashion that would later be adopted by USAAF airmen on the noses of their bombers, and it happened that, while the crew of U-99 were working-up in Kiel for their first patrol, one man noticed that a pair of horseshoes were hanging from the starboard anchor. Kretschmer accepted his 1st

Officer's suggestion that this was an omen nobody could ignore. The new insignia of U-99 would be a gilded horseshoe.

By the end of February 1941, Schepke and Kretschmer could each claim to have sunk more than 200,000 tons of Allied shipping. Indeed, most authorities credit Kretschmer with 50,000 tons more, including a destroyer and three armed merchantmen, and he was judged to be the best torpedo marksman in the German Navy. He did not subscribe to the official view that the best way to ensure a hit was to fire a fan of three or four and the proof of the pudding was that U-99 seldom came home from a *feindfahrt* without a kill. Kretschmer's method was to shadow the convoy in daylight and approach at night—if in bright moonlight from the dark side and on moonless nights from the windward side to ensure that the lookouts were facing into spray—and, then passing in between the escorts at periscope depth, to deliver his attacks from within the convoy columns.

Prien, meanwhile, had claimed over 150,000 tons. There had been an unhappy episode in an otherwise brilliant career when, in late June 1940, he torpedoed and sank, without warning, the 15,000-ton British liner *Arandora Star*, only to discover that most of the passengers were German and Italian civilians being shipped from Britain for internment in Canada.

The people of Germany, however, if not of Italy, would hear no word against their hero, for it was Prien who, shortly after midnight on 13t/14th October 1939, had crept into the Royal Navy's Orkney Islands anchorage, Scapa Flow, using all his sea-going experience to pass through the partially-blocked Kirk Sound with the rising tide, and had found the 29,000-ton *Royal Oak*, Flagship of the Home Fleet's 2nd Battle Squadron, lying at anchor. Three of his first salvo had missed, but the fourth struck home. Prien had moved away, reloaded and fired four more torpedoes. Illuminated by the eerie glow of the Aurora Borealis, the great old battleship went down in minutes. She was of World War I vintage and expendable, but the 833 officers and men who went down with her were not, and the disaster shook the Royal Navy and the British people, prompting a neutral merchant skipper justifiably to ask: "How can this happen, when the RAF have an airfield on the Orkneys?"

Prien's was a daring, skillful feat, and particularly significant for the Kriegsmarine and Germany because it was performed in the very anchorage where the Kaiser's high sea fleet had been sunk at the end of World War I—scuttled by their crews while the Allies pondered over their disposal. All aboard U-47 knew that, and while they sailed southeast from the Orkneys homeward bound, the Executive Officer, Leutnant zur See Engelbert Endrass (himself a future ace), exercised his artistic talent by decorating the conning tower with a

Erich Topp, commander of U-552, is warmly greeted on his return to Brittany from an Atlantic patrol.

The captain of
U-95 in port
at St Nazaire.

painting of a red, snorting bull—the bull, he explained, which had charged into the British Navy's haven and gored their famous battleship. It was an insignia later to be adopted by every boat in Prien's flotilla.

When U-47 tied up at Wilhelmshaven three days later, brass bands played and a multitude cheered. Grossadmiral Raeder and Admiral Dönitz marched up the gangplank, buttons gleaming on their long, dark greatcoats, and with their gold braided caps set squarely on their heads—Dönitz to embrace the commander and pin an Iron Cross (2nd class) on every crewman's chest, Raeder to shake them by the hand. That afternoon the crew were flown to Berlin in Hitler's private aircraft to be hailed by the citizens. Prien was driven through the Brandenburg Gate in an open limousine and received the sort of welcome reserved in the democracies for the heads of friendly, powerful states.

In his private office Hitler then conferred the Knight;s Cross on the hero for what he called "the proudest deed that a German U-boat could possibly carry out". Prien had done a lot more than sink a British battleship. He had made the Führer look upon the U-boat arm with a new regard and, incidentally, had won Karl Dönitz promotion to the rank of Vice Admiral. And, to the resoundingly titled Minister of Propaganda and Public Enlightenment, Doctor Josef Göbbels, the sinking of the *Royal Oak* was a gift. So overwhelming was the

publicity given to the incident that Prien was embarrassed. "Damn it", he growled. "I am an officer, not a film star." It was a manly but ingenious remark. He knew well enough that, since Scapa Flow, he was not and never would be just another German officer. The legend of the heroic, lone sea-wolf was born.

Prien, Schepke and Kretschmer soon became as popular with the German public as the RAF fighter pilots would be with the British when they fought the great air battles over southeast England in the months to come. Postcards depicting the young, smiling faces of the U-boat aces were on sale all over Europe, and stories of their exploits, sometimes with embellishments (Doctor Göbbels was not a man to underplay his hand) appeared throughout the land. Prien was persuaded to write the story of *My Road to Scapa Flow*, and Schepke produced a tract that was not so much a story as a recruiting pamphlet, chock full of Nazi propaganda, masquerading as an account of his exploits. Military bands played "The Kretschmer March" at every opportunity, but 'Silent Otto' rejected all attempts to glorify him further (unlike Schepke and many of their fellow-officers, neither he nor Prien was a Party member) and waited until the war was over before putting pen to paper.

The day, however, of the ace U-boat commander, in the role of lone raider, was drawing to a close. Britain's overdue adoption of the escorted convoy brought about a

At war's end U.S. Army personnel inspect bomb damage caused by Allied aircraft to one of the U-boat bunkers. Little significant damage was inflicted by the raiders in several attacks on the submarine pens.

change in U-boat tactics. Dönitz's dream was about to be fulfilled; the night of the wolfpack was at hand. In the early hours of 14th October 1940, Kretschmer's U-99 sailed on her fourth Atlantic patrol as one of eight boats directed by headquarters to intercept a heavily escorted westbound convoy designated SC7. The raiders found their target after four days sailing, and launched a night-long series of attacks. Stealing to and fro among the freighters and the tankers, in between the escorts, U-99 was never out of action or short of targets. Kretschmer's torpedoes and guns accounted for nine of the seventeen merchantmen sent to the bottom on that deadly night. Back in Lorient four days later, Karl Dönitz proudly described the achievement as "the greatest adventure story of the war'. But Otto Kretschmer found no great enjoyment in his later visit to Berlin, for neither meat nor alcohol was served in the Chancellery, and tobacco was strictly taboo.

The remarkable careers of Dönitz's three aces continued as members of the pack, and Hitler awarded the Knight's Cross of the Iron Cross with Oak Leaves to them all. By the end of March 1941, however, Prien and Schepke were dead and Kretschmer was a prisoner of war. Günther Prien had been on active service, with very little respite since the first days of the war when, late on 6th March, he led a pack of six boats, including Kretschmer' U-99,

in an attack on a westbound convoy out of Liverpool. In the next twenty-four hours four merchantmen were hit, and two of them went down, but the escort struck back with well-directed depth-charges. One U-boat was damaged and limped home to Lorient, another was abandoned and scuttled by the crew. Kretschmer, for once, saw discretion as the better part of valour, and left the scene of action, but Prien would not let the convoy go. He trailed it until the evening of 8th March and was closing on a target when a break in the showers he was using as a screen revealed his position to the destroyer HMS Wolverine. Prien crash-dived but his boat was badly damaged; when he surfaced an hour later, Wolverine was waiting.

The hero of Scapa Flow made his final dive. A doubt remains as to whether he was sent down by the Royal Navy or by another U-boat's maverick torpedo, but U-47, with its snorting bull insignia, exploded just below the surface and there were no survivors.

Ten days later, as Lieutenant Commander Peter Kemp put it in Purnell's History of the Second World War, "Schepke took too many liberties with a convoy escort". When U-100's wake was spotted from the bridge of the destroyer Walker, Captain Donald Macintyre gave chase and dropped a pattern of depth-charges at the point where Schepke had submerged. No result was evident, and Walker turned back to pick up the survivors from one of the four freighters the U-boats had torpedoed. Within half an hour, the newly-installed radar on *Walker*'s sister ship, HMS *Vanoc*, had found the U-100, lying on the surface while Schepke inspected the damage caused by the depth-charges. The speeding destroyer then rammed the U-boat amidships, and her crew were either flung or jumped into the water. Schepke was standing on the bridge from which he had dealt out so much death and destruction when *Vanoc*'s bows sliced his legs off at the thigh; as the destroyer went astern to extricate herself, what remained of Schepke, arms flailing wildly, was torn free of the conning tower and flung into the sea. He, with U-100 and forty-nine of her crew, disappeared beneath the swell. While *Walker* maintained an Asdic sweep around her, *Vanoc* moved in to pick up the five survivors.

Within half an hour, the two destroyers had yet another Asdic contact: they did not know it, but they had found the ace of aces. Their depth-charges damaged the hull and both the propellers of Otto Kretschmer's U-99 and drove him down to the dangerous depth of 700 feet. When at last he had to surface, the boat lay tilted heavily to starboard, with no torpedoes left and no means of manoeuve, as helpless as a beached whale. On HMS *Walker*, Captain Macintyre now trained his guns on the super-

structure, intending to force the crew to abandon ship and to take the U-boat in one piece. Kretschmer, however, was determined he should not: lighting a cigar in the shelter of the conning tower, he ordered his men to don their warmest clothes and to open all the hatches. The stem went under, and men on the afterdeck were washed into the sea.

Otto Kretschmer signalled to Macintyre by lamp: "Captain to captain, please pick up my men in the water who are drifting towards you. I am sinking." Gratefully, Kretschmer saw the destroyer's crew prepare to lower a boat. Still the conning tower with the famous golden horseshoe stayed above the waves. An engineer asked the captain's leave to go below and flood the ballast tanks. At last U-99 went down, and the engineer with her, as did two more of the crew. Treading water, the remainder held hands in an attempt to ensure no more were swept away. A scrambling net was lowered from *Walker*'s deck, and the U-boat men climbed aboard. Kretschmer, now exhausted and with his sea-boots filled with water, could only cling to the netting until his bosun came along to help. Repeatedly Lorient radioed U-99 and U-100: "Report your position." The calls went unanswered and unheard.

On 21st March Walker docked in Liverpool: the crew of U-99 were handed over to the Army and

A pair of Type VII U-boats are accommodated
for shelter in this Brittany base bunker.

their commander was taken to London for interrogation. He was interviewed there by Captain George Creasy RN, commanding the Royal Navy's Anti-Submarine Divsion, who later recorded his impressions in the book *The Golden Horseshoe*, Terence Robertson's excellent biography of Kretschmer: "He gave nothing away. I saw a young and obviously self-confident naval commander who bore himself, in the difficult circumstances of recent capture, with self-respect, modesty and courtesy."

Kretschmer was informed by his captors that he had been promoted to the rank of Lieutenant Commander with effect 1st March (as had Prien posthoumously), and that the Swords had been added to the Oak Leaves of his Knight's Cross. Men who had sailed with and learned from him made their presence felt in the North Atlantic long after he had been put 'behind the wire'. The last word about him must be with his captor, Captain Macintyre: "Compared with his exhuberant fellow aces he seemed a sinister figure. Out in the wastes of the North Atlantic he and U-99 were indeed a sinister and deadly menace."

In the space of only ten days, Dönitz had lost three of his best and bravest commanders.

Otto Kretschmer, on his release from imprisonment in 1947, returned to peacetime duties in the

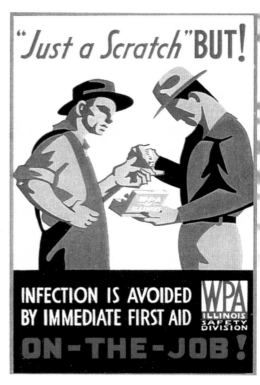

Posters of the U.S. war effort.

German Navy and, as Konteradmiral Kretschmer, became Chief of Staff to the NATO forces, Baltic Approaches. Later, at a pleasant gathering in England, Captain Donald Macintyre shook his former prisoner's hand and then returned the fine Zeiss binoculars that he had 'borrowed' from Kretschmer in 1941.

". . . he wanted to prove he could attack by night on the surface and carry out his personal principle of "one torpedo, one ship". "Fans of torpedoes were, in his opinion, a waste of equipment and effort and allowed a U-boat commander to attack from a position of comparative safety in the hope of hitting something, instead of taking carefully calculated risks and by precision firing making evey torpedo count. It was from this time that he became the first commander to attack convoys only by night and always on the surface. This attack was to set the pattern. At this stage of the war no other commanders followed Kretschmer's technique, considering it too dangerous, yet it was this method that led him to outstrip his colleagues at sinkings."
—from *The Golden Horseshoe* by Terence Robertson

"No more striking measure of the strong sense of security against U-boats which dominated all minds at Scapa Flow can be found than in the fact that, after one torpedo from the first volley had actually struck the *Royal Oak* none of the vigilant and experienced officers conceived that it could be a torpedo. The danger from the air was the one first apprehended, and large numbers of the crew took up their air-raid stations under the armour, and were thereby doomed, while at the same time the captain and admiral were examining alternative possibilities of an internal explosion. It was in these conditions that the second volley of torpedoes was discharged. Thus the forfeit has been claimed, and we mourn the loss of 800 gallant officers and men and, of a ship which, although very old, was of undoubted military value."
—Winston Churchill

"I was astounded to see the food supply for eight weeks disappear between pipes and valves, ribs and machines, closets and ducts. Huge smoked hams were hung in the control room. Staples such as whipped cream, butter, coffee and tea were locked up for distribution by the Captain. The fueling of U-557 was accomplished on May 10. On May 12 we received loads of fresh vegetables, eggs, bread and fresh water. We squeezed the crisp loaves into the last unoccupied crannies and filled three hammocks with the rest, letting them swing free in the bow and aft compartments."
—from *Iron Coffins* by Herbert A. Werner

The life of a U-boat man at sea consisted of two parts—on watch and off watch. The duration of these phases depended on his trade: a technician stood two watches of six hours each, and a seaman three of four hours—from midnight to four o'clock, and so on through the day. Only the cook was excused the watch, and that was with good reason: he had to produce three meals a day for each of the watches, and that important duty, constantly interrupted by the movement of his crew mates through the narrow galley, was enough to keep him busy for every waking hour.

The First and Second Lieutenants, and the navigator or quartermaster (usually a Chief Petty Officer) each stood a watch in turn, accompanied by a Petty Officer and two seamen. The four-hour deck-watch would probably be halved in the very worst of weather, when big seas swept the decks in solid sheets of water, and the rain came at the bridge horizontally, vertically and diagonally. In these conditions no amount of clothing—neither oilskin coats and leather trousers, sou'westers over Balaclava helmets, double pairs of socks inside the sea-boots, nor sweaters with towels wrapped round the neck—could prevent a man from being frozen to the marrow and soaked to the skin within minutes of taking up his post. It was in that sort of weather, aided by a sudden gale, that the entire deck-watch of U-106 was swept

Kriegsmarine lookouts on a routine
Atlantic convoy patrol.

away by a monster wave. No one was aware of it until a control room hand had cause to go aloft.

A U-boat crewman, like a flier in a heavy bomber, lived a life that combined similar but unequal periods of boredom and tedium, terror and excitement. The difference lay in the time scale: the flier measured his in hours and minutes, the seaman in weeks and hours. In a way, the on-and-off watch routine could be reassuring: each man knew his duty and where he had to be at any time of day or night. It could also be maddening in its sameness and predictability: hour after hour of staring at horizons, listening through headphones, recharging batteries, watching dials and gauges, greasing, cleaning and, when not so occupied, peeling potatoes. Even the diversions—the fire drills, the escape drills, trim-test dives, practice with the guns, simulated crash-dives with the officers taking turns—even these became matters of tedious routine.

When the boat was on the surface in a choppy sea, with the induction valves closed to keep the water out and the diesel engines breathing inboard air, the inboard atmosphere was stifling and the temperature could rise to 120 degrees Fahrenheit. Fresh water was only available for drinking and cooking; no one shaved unless the commander was a crank, and nobody bathed except in a bucket, perhaps for months on end. Clothes stank of sweat and diesel

clockwise from top left: The captain on his conning tower; A crewman drenched from the tower hatch; Target sighting in the Atlantic battle; Survival training preparatory to going on patrol.

oil, and no amount of washing could ever make them clean. Grey shirts were favoured because they did not advertise the dirt. To mitigate the smells, men dabbed lemon cologne on salt-caked faces, rubbed fragrant waters in greasy, matted hair and used oily unguents to cleanse dirty skin. Despite the help of pills and castor oil, constipation was endemic; teeth and gums suffered from the lack of skilled attention and gingivitis was a chronic ailment. Not many crewmen retained all their teeth for very long.

Whenever the boat rose to the surface after being submerged, per-haps for many hours, a dirty yellow cloud would flow out of the conning tower, and a queue of seamen would form in the control room below the open hatch, holding up their pallid faces to inhale the clean sea air, and waiting for permission to take a turn on deck; there they could relieve their aching bladders into the wide Atlantic and perhaps enjoy a cigarette: an indulgence that, unlike their British counterparts, they were normally denied within the boat.

The eyes of the U-boat were on the bridge, where the men on watch, like the gunners in a bomber's tur-rets, maintained an ever-roving eye: sideways and back across their sec-tor of the ocean as far as the horizon, up, down and around the piece of sky above. As with many of the gunners in bombers flying by day, the watch into sunlight was not only the most taxing on the eyes, they faced the direction from which a combat-wise attacker was most likely to approach.

The word from the Admiral was: "He who sees first has won", and all around the compass, any sort of sighting had to be checked. Was that a lump of nimbo-stratus dead ahead or a smudge of smoke from an approaching warship's stacks? Was that a seagull on the starboard quarter at 200 feet or a Catalina flying boat at 4,000? Up with the binoculars again— binoculars that seemed to weigh more by the hour. Those people in the Zeiss factory clearly never had to take a sea-watch.

For the men on watch, there was little time to marvel at the spectacle of twilight or dawn, or at the ever-changing spectrum of colours, light and shade that came between. It was not for them to enjoy the summer evenings when the decks seemed to be gilded, nor to wonder at the savage splendour of a great electric storm, when jagged streaks of lightning flashed between the ocean and the lurid sky; they could not allow themselves to gaze at Aurora Borealis, spectrally glinting in the northern sky, not at the distant beauty of the constellations overhead. Any such deviance from strict concentration was sure to be noticed by the officer of the watch, and to earn a sharp reproof.

If the U-boat's eyes were on the bridge and its heart in the control room, its ears were in the radio and hydrophone shacks and its sinews in

top left: A cook at work on a Type VII boat; above: torpedo "mixers" readying their charges for action in the north Atlantic; left: The helmsman of a Type VII U-boat.

the engine room. When the boat submerged it was entirely blind, and then only the sound waves, coming through the headphones from an array of microphones fixed underneath the bows, could give warning of vessels within range. The 'sound man' could read the vessel's bearing and judge whether it was closing or moving away: in optimum conditions, on the quarters of the beam, he could detect a single ship at a distance of about twelve miles, and the sound of a convoy could be heard at sixty. When the U-boat was submerged, he was one man who always had the ear of the commander. On the surface, the hydrophone was ineffective, and when the boat was snorkelling, the roar of the engines blotted out all sound. Aft in the engine room, with the diesels running, the noise was absolutely deafening, and the mechanics used their own sign language for communication.

The radio telegraphist came into action when the boat was on the surface and short-wave messages could be transmitted and received. Then, it was his task to send reports of attacks and counterattacks to BdU—U-boat headquarters— with the boat's position, its torpedo and fuel states, the sea conditions and the weather, and to receive deployment orders in return; between times he would listen in on signals sent from other U-boats in the wolfpack and, whenever possible, eavesdrop on messages from the merchant ships.

Thoughtful commanders (and Kapitänleutnant Otto Kretschmer was one such) routinely submerged for two hours or so before dawn, with two purposes in mind. First, to facilitate the use of the hydrophone and so avoid collision with vessels that might approach unnoticed in the dark; and second, being mindful of the stresses on the crew, to allow them to relax, get cleaned up and eat their breakfast undisturbed. Mealtimes on the surface, especially in rough weather, tended to be messy affairs; food in transit from the galley sometimes failed to reach its destination in one piece, and the guard rails, or 'fiddles' fitted to tables, might save the crockery but

The captain and crewmen of the U-boat
in the film *Das Boot* experiencing a depth-
charge attack; above: Gauges in the sub
U-995 on display at Laboe, Germany; left:
The Zeiss binoculars of a World War Two
U-boat commander.

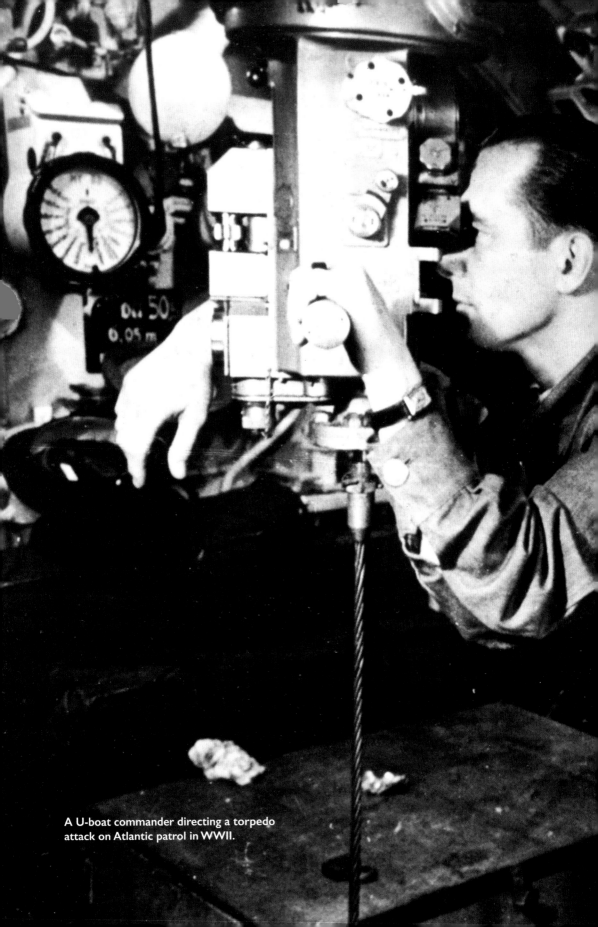

A U-boat commander directing a torpedo attack on Atlantic patrol in WWII.

not always the contents.

Kretschmer's fellow commander, Günther Prien, could be less considerate. He had a degree of arrogance that was sometimes evident in young men of his breeding and was no great disadvantage in the role that he sustained throughout his brilliant career, although it might not have made him welcome in a Royal Navy wardroom. As an example of his style, he would order harbour exercises for his crew in between patrols, in which he did not join. His crew respected him, but there was no need to love him. The public did love him, but they did not really know him and Dönitz, who favoured him, never had to sail with him.

Under water, the U-boat moved moved smoothly and almost in silence; on the surface it pitched and tossed with the motion of the sea, rearing onto great wave crests and swooping into troughs, twisting and rolling in the cross seas; the rhythmic pounding of the diesels, the singing of the jumping wire on the foredeck and the constant slap of waves against the hull were sounds as eternally monotonous as, to an airman, were the growl of the aero-engines, the whistle of the aerials, and the howl of slipstream tearing at the fuselage.

However stalwart he might be through attacks from the air or from the sea, however hardy in the freezing hours on watch, the U-boat sailor's morale could be sapped by

Merchant ship victims of Kreigs-
marine torpedoes; right: A wash
from a pan among the torpedo
tubes of this boat on WWII patrol.

the infuriating, constantly repeated habits of his mess-mates. There was the radio man who played the same dreary waltz tune by the hour on the phonograph, and there was the stoker who, at every meal, picked his teeth with a table fork. And as if human behaviour were not annoying enough, three or four French flies, a thousand miles from base, were always there at meal-times and when a man was trying to sleep, somehow evading every swipe, and providing an irritating lesson in the art of survival to everyone on board.

Conversation in the crew's quarters tended to be rough, even obscene, as it always has been and will probably always be among servicemen. Sexual experiences, real or imagined, were described in detail and at length, liaisons planned for the next return to port lasciviously envisaged, Winston Churchill was routinely reviled, desk-bound officers of the flotilla staff were savagely derided, and even the Führer did not escape calumny (although woe betide the officer who was openly critical of the Hitler regime. As in any close-knit group, jesting insults were frequently exchanged, usually accepted in the spirit they were meant and as pointedly returned, but on occasion a remark would cause disproportionate and rankling offence.

From the early days of 1943 the crew could listen on various frequencies and several times a week, to broadcasts by one "Commander

left: Manning the gun with the deck awash; below: Loading a torpedo in Brittany; bottom: Relaxing briefly in crew quarters aboard a submarine.

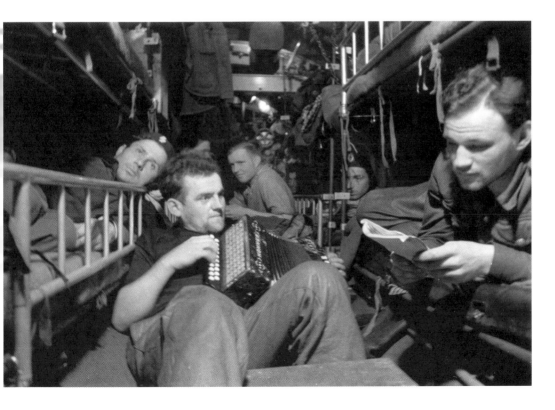

Robert Lee Norden" (the *nom de guerre* of a German-speaking U.S. Navy officer). He would tell them of appalling losses in the U-boat arm, giving names and numbers, and describe how ill-advisedly their campaign was led as well as mentioning disgusting scandals among the Nazi Party hierarchy, insisting how well off all would be but for Adolf Hitler's insane lust for conquest. This was all seemingly backed up by solid evidence, and spoken soberly as if by a friend. The British had been waging a similar war of words from "Radio Atlantic", which while purporting to emanate from a resistance movement in the heart of Germany, was actually being broadcast from the Duke of Bedford's stately home at Woburn Abbey. Both propaganda efforts attracted a wide audience, in the same way as William Joyce, or "Lord Haw Haw", talking from Berlin, drew many Britons to their wireless sets, sometimes for the sheer fun of it, and sometimes to say "Blimey, he's right, you know!"

To maintain a high morale among men who are liable to be killed at any time, but who must be persuaded to carry on the fight, has always been a problem and a test of leadership. Any attempt to conceal or minimize the danger will soon be seen as false, and mistrust of the leader will surely follow; history has shown that sometimes the best course is to state the danger plainly, and say "whatever is to come, we'll face it together, and in the end we'll win." That was how Winston Churchill inspired and heartened the British people in their darkest hour, with his open acknowledgement that "blood, toil, tears and sweat" would precede their victory.

For the Anglo-Saxon races, if not for the Teutonic, a leavening of humour, possibly macabre, has often been helpful in living through adversity, as music hall comedians and press cartoonists have long known. The fighting man employs and enjoys this kind of humour, but he needs something more to maintain his spirit and stiffen his resolve; at times he is sustained by knowing that his target is attainable, that what is asked of him is possible, and that his life will not be wasted in a hopeless cause.

The good U-boat commander was well aware of the requirement for occasional respites from the maddening routine, as any able leader should be. He would try to ensure that the boat's library was adequately stocked, that someone aboard could play the accordion or the harmonica, that the stock of phonograph records were of a sort the seamen liked; if someone had a birthday he would throw an *ad hoc* party in the fore-ends , with the cook's best effort at a cake, a bottle of beer and perhaps a little cognac. Such simple small diversions could be like shafts of sunlight piercing heavy cloud; they could encourage the belief that normal life went on, even in that strange world below the sea.

above: Lookouts scanning
the horizon for possible target
vessels.

The unpleasant rolling of a U-boat on the surface of a rough sea; top right: A U-boat engineer tends his diesels; right: At rest in. the forward torpedo room of the Type VII.

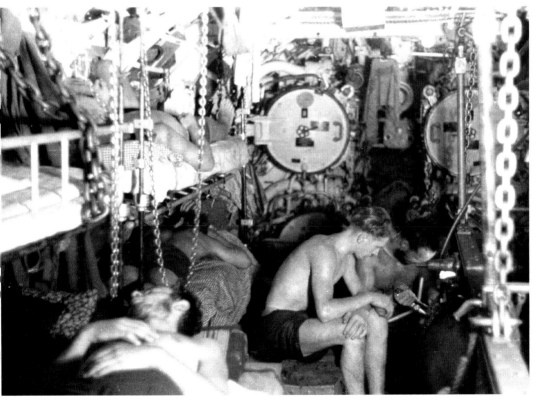

"Shipboard routine had replaced the excitement of the chase and the battle. And it was a maddening routine. The small ship rolled and slapped, listed and shuddered endlessly. Utensils, spare parts, tools, and conserves showered down on us continually; porcelain cups and dishes shattered on the deck plates and in the bilges as we ate our meals directly out of cans. The men, penned up together in the rocking, sweating drum, took the motion and the monotony with stoicism. Occasionally, someone's temper flared, but spirits remained high. We were all patient veterans. Everyone aboard looked alike, smelled alike, had adopted the same phrases and curses. We had learned to live together in a narrow tube no longer than two railroad cars. We tolerated each other's faults and became experts on each other's habits—how everyone laughed and snarled, talked and snored, sipped his coffee and caressed his beard. The pressure mounted with the passage of each uneventful day, but it could be relieved in an instant by the sight of a fat convoy."
—from *Iron Coffins*
by Herbert A. Werner

"A gossip is one who talks to you about others; a bore is one who talks to you about himself; and a brilliant conversationalist is one who talks to you about yourself."
—Lisa Kirk
New York Journal American

right: Among the sausages and bread loaves, a U-boat crewman writes a letter home.

BUNDLES FOR BRITAIN

The Merchant Sailor memorial at Halifax, Nova Scotia.

Britain never has been a self-supporting nation. She has always needed a volume of imports to survive, and in time of war it is the Royal Navy's task to keep the sea lanes open for the exchange of trade. In the 1930s, a third of Britain's food, including most of her meat, butter, cheese and wheat, came from overseas sources, while for home-grown crops British farmers depended on imported fertilizers. Much of her steel and timber came from North America, and other essential materials were imported from all over the world: wool from Australasia, nitrates from South America, iron ore from Norway and Africa, cotton from the Americas, Egypt and India, rubber from Malaya, zinc and lead from North America and Australia, and oil from the USA, Persia and the Dutch West Indies. Three thousand merchant ships—freighters and tankers—were needed to carry the more than four million tons of resources that Britain needed every month.

In World War I the Kaiser's U-boats had brought the British people to the brink of starvation and would have achieved their aim but for the efforts of the Royal Navy, with massive assistance from America. Dönitz knew all about that long campaign, and he was determined to do better the next time round. The primary target for the U-boat arm had to be not Britain's warships (although they would always be prime bonus targets), but the merchant shipping, without which her people could neither eat, run their industries nor continue fighting. Empty or laden, those ships must be sunk.

Although, at the start of World War II, the Royal Navy was not what it had been twenty years before—the policy of disarmament in the early 1930s had made sure of that—it still equalled the strength of any other navy and was formidable enough to deter Hitler's admirals from contemplating the sort of set-piece battles that for old sea-dogs were the only proper way to fight a war. Grossadmiral Raeder was forced to agree that a prime target for the Kriegsmarine had to be British imports from wherever they might come.

Despite the havoc wrought on merchant shipping by the U-boats during World War I, the Royal Navy appeared to have forgotten most of the lessons learned. The First Sea Lord, for example, considered that the major threat would come from German surface warships, and even his superior, Winston Churchill, as First Lord of the Admiralty, pronounced that the U-boats' early successes "need not cause any undue despondency or alarm". The requirement for organized convoys, with naval protection, as practiced by Britain since the 14th century, and as demanded by Churchill himself in the early days of World War I for ships carrying troops and freight from Australasia to Europe, was largely ignored when World War II began.

A slow ship sailing singly, like a heavy bomber flying alone, once it was detected, was always easy prey, whereas ships in convoy and bombers in formation could offer some degree of mutual protection and support. The speed of a convoy, however, was limited to that of the slowest vessel in it, and like large air formations, convoys were slow and awkward to manoeuvre in evasive action. As the RAF knew, and the USAAF was to learn, bomber formations needed fighter escorts if they were to reach their targets and return. The same was true of convoys—they needed warships to protect them, or at least to discourage their attackers. Statistics showed that, on the sea or in the air, the straggling or stricken craft was always more likely to be downed.

From the Royal Navy's point of view, convoy escort was not the most sought after of duties; furthermore, there were not enough suitable vessels or trained crews to undertake it. The fact that air cover was almost non-existent until 1941 was not at all surprising since the RAF, like the Home Fleet, was crucially engaged in the defence of Britain from the German invasion—Operation Sealion—and also in trying to take the war to Germany, albeit with bombers not far short of obsolescence. Furthermore, the degree of co-operation between the two services was not what it might have been, and it would be two long years before the Navy and the Air Force brought themselves fully to co-operate in protecting merchant

shipping. In the early days, the Navy's Fleet Air Arm flew many gallant sorties against the German surface ships, taking off in single-engined Fairey Swordfish biplanes—"Stringbags" to their crews—from flight decks grafted onto freighters. Their navigation was by compass, rule and sextant, and their aircraft lacked the range, the armament and the effecive search radar sets to hunt and fight the U-boats.

Meanwhile, the convoys formed and put bravely out to sea. The so-called "fast" convoys were by no means fast, and the slow convoys were very slow indeed. Sailing at an average nine knots, a "fast" convoy's passage time from North America to one of Britain's southwest ports was usually rather more than fifteen days; the slow ships took some four or five days more, and the convoys that formed at Freetown on the west coast of North Africa took about the

The darkened interior of a pen at the Bordeaux U-bunker.

same. Once France had fallen, Hitler's Axis partner Benito Mussolini began to threaten the Mediterranean, and shipping from the east had to take the long route round the Cape of Good Hope into the Atlantic—a passage time of many weeks.

Apart from the difficulties of mustering the vessels at the port of departure, of fuelling and provisioning them, of ensuring that they sailed together, stayed in position and main-

tained communication, the convoy system had certain other problems. One was that the installations at the ports of destination were intended for the regular day-by-day arrival of ships for berthing and unloading, not for the reception of thirty or forty vessels at a time. Another problem lay in the character of the merchant skippers, a sturdy and independent breed of men accustomed to taking orders only from their owners. In the opinion of

one Royal Navy officer, who spoke from experience, the sinkings of merchant ships would have been far fewer if only their masters had done what they were told. None of this concerned the U-boat commanders: they simply wanted to find them, torpedo them, and leave them and their cargoes on the bottom of the sea; if their crews went down with them, *c'est la guerre*. In June 1940, food rationing in Britain was already strict,

while with access to the produce of all the conquered nations—Poland, Czechoslovakia, Denmark, Sweden, Norway, Belgium, the Netherlands, and France—Germany would never starve: the stubborn British in their islands surely would.

For their part, the British did not see it in that light. In the Submarine Tracking Room at the British Admiralty, U-boat positions, as indicated by whatever sources were available:

The Liberty ship, *Jeremiah O'Brien*, a survivor of the Second World War, now moored in San Francisco bay.

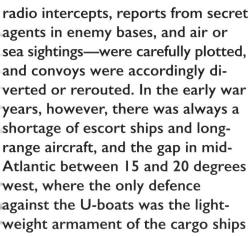

radio intercepts, reports from secret agents in enemy bases, and air or sea sightings—were carefully plotted, and convoys were accordingly diverted or rerouted. In the early war years, however, there was always a shortage of escort ships and long-range aircraft, and the gap in mid-Atlantic between 15 and 20 degrees west, where the only defence against the U-boats was the light-weight armament of the cargo ships

themselves, was known to the seamen of the Merchant Navy as "The Graveyard", and to the Ubootwaffe as "The Black Pit".

The life of the merchant seamen had never been an easy one. They were accustomed to its harshness and austerity; they had learned how to make a meal out of corned beef and hard tack; how to catch a few hours sleep between their watches, if only on a locker top; and how to

the Great Lakes of North America, along with various ancient vessels reclaimed from the scrapyard. The majority were British, while some flew neutral flags—Swedish, Greek and Norwegian. Their cargoes were steel, timber, oil, grain, iron ore and sulphur, and they were escorted by a 1,000-ton Royal Navy sloop, HMS *Scarborough*, armed with depth-charges and two four-inch guns. They would also be accompanied, for the first two days, by a seaplane and, less encouragingly, by an armed yacht. The convoy commodore was to be Vice Admiral Lachlan Mackinnon of the Royal Naval Reserve, who would fly his flag in the Liverpool-based cargo ship *Assyrian*, which, ironically, had been built in Hamburg at the start of World War I.

On the first day at sea one of the Lake ships turned back with mechanical problems, and it was replaced on the Sunday by *Shekatika*, a large British steamer that had failed to keep pace with a preceding convoy sailing out of Halifax. The formation, rectangular in shape and covering some five square miles of ocean, made up three five-ship columns, one headed by *Assyrian*, and five four-ship columns with the longer columns stationed in the centre. The thinking was that, since U-boat attacks came mainly from abeam, the convoy's profile presented a minimal target and that the columns in the middle, where the tankers were stationed, were less likely to be attacked.

At dawn on the sixth day, in heavy

live with the impossibility of ever being dry. Now, however, they faced the threat of being torpedoed, mined and machine-gunned a thousand miles from land.

For them, the most fearful days of World War II were in the summer and autumn of 1940—the period that came to be known in the U-boat arm as "die glückliche Zeit". It was at the height of this "happy time", on Saturday, 5th October, that convoy SC7 sailed from Sydney, Cape Breton Island, Nova Scotia, en route for the Clyde. SC7 was the seventh of the slower convoys—those with a speed of just six or seven knots— and it consisted of thirty-five ships, including three designed for sailing

Few bodies of water generate more violence and terror than the roiling seas of the North Atlantic where American, British and Canadian corvettes hunted German subs in the historic Battle of the Atlantic.

A Liberty ship is escorted in convoy by American and British warships; right: Jack Hawkins in a scene from the motion picture *The Cruel Sea*.

seas, the remaining Lake steamers and two of the Greek ships were nowhere to be seen. Five days later, far off course to the south, and 27 miles astern, the Canadian Lake steamer *Trevisa* was torpedoed and sunk by the patrolling Kapitänleutnant Wilhelm Schultze in U-124. Six of *Trevisa*'s crew went down with her, and it was only by good fortune that the destroyer HMS *Keppel* came alongside in time to rescue the remainder.

On Thursday, 17th October, twelve days into the voyage, the convoy had made its slow way past longitude 57 degrees north and was just off the southern coast of Iceland, when it came within the sight of Korvetten-

kapitän Heinrich Bleichrodt on the bridge of U-48. Bleichrodt passed the news by short-wave radio to BdU in Lorient. Six other U-boats were within twelve hours sailing of that part of the Atlantic. U-99 and U-100, respectively commanded by the aces Otto Kretschmer and Joachim Schepke, Heinrich Liebe's U-38, Karl-Heinz Mohle's U-123, Fritz Frauen-heim's U-101, and U-46, with Günther Prien's erstwhile Ist Lieutenant En-gelbert Endrass, in command. Dönitz then ordered them to form a bar-rier—a "stripe" as he called it—and to 'mark time' across and forward of the convoy's course to the east of Rockall, the tiny island outcrop in the North Atlantic drift. Bleichrodt, how-

ever, decided not to wait. He launched his attack at four o'clock in the morning, and his aim was deadly: with three torpedoes, he destroyed the freighters *Corinthic* and *Scoresby*, and the 10,000-ton French tanker *Languedoc*. The escorting *Scarborough*, now joined by her sister sloop *Fowey* and the corvette *Bluebell* from Britain, picked up such survivors as they found.

Attacked by the escort, and later by a Sunderland flying boat, Bleichrodt lost contact and resumed his patrol, while his telegraphist signalled a report of the action back to BdU. Captain Dickinson, sailing in *Scarborough* learned by radio of the Sundeland crew's sighting and showed fine fight-ing spirit, if not good judgement, by making his best speed to the position as reported. He hunted U-48 for twenty-four hours, but he failed to find her, and was of no further help to convoy SC7.

In the early light of Friday, 18th October, Liebe was the first of the reinforcements to arrive, and he was joined in the evening by the other five. Chancing on the straggling Greek grain ship *Aenos* while en route, Liebe had stopped her with a torpedo and sunk her by gunfire, but that was the limit of his success. The rest of the wolfpack, however, was in luck. They found the convoy, keeping good formaion north of Rockall and making southeast for the Clyde.

DON'T WASTE BREAD !

SAVE TWO SLICES EVERY DAY and
Defeat the 'U' Boat

When Endrass in U-46 launched the first attack at 8:15 pm, Commander Robert Sherwood was on the bridge of *Bluebell*. "Suddenly", he said, "it was 'bang, bang,, bang, and the place was lit up like Piccadilly Circus." For the rest of that night, despite every effort by the escort, now joined by the sloop *Leith* and the corvette *Heartsease*, the U-boats created havoc in a perfect textbook demonstration of the wolfpack tactics—*die rudeltaktik*—envisaged by their Admiral.

The light of a full moon shining through the drifts of cloud showed a dreadful panorama of floating wreckage, some of it still burning under palls of smoke, of flaming oil slicks, and of drifing lifeboats, some empty and others full of men. Among them

the escort vessels speeded to and fro, the gunners firing "snowflake" starshells which, although they might illuminate a U-boat, provided the same service for the enemy and could temporarily blind the lookout on a merchantman at a crucial moment. Once a torpedo, intended for a freighter, with its depth set for a vessel of that draft, passed directly below the keel of *Leith*, whose decks were taking on the appearance of a floating casualty station.

The Swedish vessel *Convallaria* with her load of pulp wood was sunk by U-46's torpedoes and she was followed to the bottom by the Cardiff ship *Beautus*, carrying steel and timber. Against the commodore's instructions, the Dutch ship *Boekolo* slowed to save the crew of *Beautus* and, for her pains, was herself sunk. *Shekatika* went down, as did *Creekirk* with her crew and cargo of iron ore. Next to go was *Empire Miniver*, the biggest vessel in the convoy, then *Fiscus*, blown to pieces in an instant with her cargo of steel, followed qjuickly by the 1,500-ton Swedish *Gunborg* laden with pulp wood. Again, defying the orders, but obeying their human. instincts, the Greeks on *Niritos* turned about to pick up *Gunborg*'s crew. The latter, however, preferred the comparative safety of their lifeboats—a reaction not totally unknown in their circumstance. They waved the old Greek ship away, and on this occasion they were tragically right: barely ten minutes later, they heard the detonation and saw the

In both world wars, government posters exhorted Americans to conserve food and eat wisely and sensibly.

EAT MORE
CORN, OATS AND RYE PRODUCTS — FISH AND POULTRY — FRUITS, VEGETABLES AND POTATOES BAKED, BOILED AND BROILED FOODS

EAT LESS
WHEAT, MEAT, SUGAR AND FATS

TO SAVE FOR THE ARMY AND OUR ALLIES

R. M. S "LUSITANIA"   SATURDAY, JUNE 27, 1914

Menu

Hors d'œuvres—Variés
Canapé—Levasseur   Tartelettes—Moscovite

Chicken Okra   Crême Algerienne

Sea Bass—Egyptienne   Fried Filet of Flounder

Grenadins á la Florentine   Biscantins—St. Germain

Sirloin & Ribs of Beef
Haunch of Mutton—Boulangére   Turkey—Mephisto
York Ham & Spinach—Sherry Sauce

Green Peas   Rice   Fried Egg Plant
Boiled, Mashed & Persillées Potatoes

Asperges—Sauce Divine
Salade de Saison

Pouding Normande
Gâteau Vanille   Petits Fours   Rhubarb Tart
Gelée au Madere

Lemon & Coffee Ices

Dessert   Café

TO ORDER FROM THE GRILL (15 Minutes)
Sirloin Steaks   Spring Chicken   Mutton Chops

vivid flames as *Niritos* with her load of sulphur, met her end. When the U-boats broke off their first attack, nine ships of the convoy had gone down in two hours.

The next assault began at midnight when the flagship *Assyrian* and half her complemen went down, sunk by torpedoes from Frauenheim's U-101. Captain Kearon and Commodore MacKinnon were two of the survivors that were pulled out of the water by the crew of *Leith*. *Blairspey*, meanwhile, was torpedoed and abandoned. Downed in turn were the old *Empire Brigade*, the Dutch tramp *Soesterberg*, the Norwegian timber ship *Snefield*,

left: A menu from RMS *Lusitania*, sunk by Kapitanleutnant Walther Schwieger and the crew of the submarine U-20 while sailing from New York to Liverpool on 6 May 1915, off Ireland.

the large British steamer *Sedgepool* and the Greek 10,000-ton *Thalia* with another precious load of steel. The *Clintonia*'s gun crew fought a brave but hopeless battle with two surfaced U-boats before they first torpedoed her and then blew her decks to pieces with their guns. When daylight broke on 19th October, only fifteen vessels of SC7 were afloat, and two of those were damaged. Throughout the action, just one U-boat was attacked by an escort and this was without effect.

Leith raced around the shambles, her decks packed with men plucked from the sea, some injured, some dying, all soaked and frozen to the bone. The sloop's young surgeon Lieutenant strove successfullt to save the life of Commodore MacKinnon, who, at the age of fifty-seven had suffered greatly from the hours spent clinging to a pit-prop in the icy water.

Command of what was left of SC7 was passed by signal to Captain Thompson, the master of *Somerby*, and the convoy limped on towards the Clyde. Somehow *Blairspey* had survived the impact of three torpedoes, and five days later the ocean rescue tug *Salvonia*, sailing out of Campbelltown, found her, reeling like a drunkard, and towed her into Gourock. *Leith* put into Liverpool and her cargo of survivors were billeted all around the city, where German bombers made them welcome with an all-night raid. At least the surviving officers would con-

A North Atlantic convoy under way
in WWII; right and far right: Merchant
Navy men; A comic book with a
U-boat theme.

tinue to be paid. Not so the seamen. It was one of the anomalies of Merchant Navy life that they came off the payroll when their ship was sunk.

Meanwhile, some 250 miles away, convoy HX79 out of Halifax was entering the Western Approaches with forty-nine cargo ships, two armed merchant cruisers, a Dutch submarine stationed in the centre of the convoy's six columns, and with the 5,000-ton *Loch Lomond* as a rescue boat. In the Western Approaches the escort was reinforced by the destroyers *Whitehall* and *Sturdy*, a mine-sweeper, four corvettes and three anti-submarine trawlers. So protected, HX79 sailed at a steady eight knots into the master sights of Dönitz's wolfpack.

Kretschmer and three more of SC7s attackers had expended their torpedoes and were sailing home, but Endrass's U-46 and Schepke's U-100 were still on station, as was Bleichrodt in U-48 with one torpedo left, and these three were joined by Liebe in U-38. It was Günther Prien, though, on patrol in U-47, who first identified HX79. Also low on torpedoes, he shadowed the convoy and called the others in. The wolfpack assembled during the evening of Saturday 19th October, and Liebe opened their attack at 9:45 pm, sinking the British steamer *Matheran*. Two freighters went down, followed by the tanker *Shirak*, whose crew of thirty-seven were rescued by the trawler *Blackfly*. The tanker *Caprella*

We risk our lives to bring you food. It's up to you not to waste it.

"A Message from our Seamen"

BUNDLES FOR BRITAIN

was sliced in two, and the motorship *Wandby*, hit by one of Prien's last torpedoes, was flooded in the engine room and had to be abandoned with her 1,500-ton cargo of pig-iron and timber.

The convoy commodore ordered a dog-leg—forty degrees to starboard for thirty minutes and eighty degrees to port for a similar period to get back on course—but the wolfpack followed them relentlessly. Some engineers from the abandoned *Wandby* volunteered to board the stricken tanker *Sitala*, which had been holed by Schepke on the starboard side forward but was still afloat and apparently seaworthy. The engi-

left: A torpedoed Merchant Navy vessel; below: On the conning tower of a German submarine following its sinking of an Allied cargo ship in the Atlantic battle.

neers got steam up and set course for England, but when the wind freshened in the night her bow planes failed to take the strain, and the armed trawler *Angle* rushed up to save the men on board. A torpedo accounted for *Whitford Point* with her steel cargo of 8,000 tons; her Chief Officer, her bosun and a fireman were the sole survivors. With horrid irony, the last casualty, at 7:25 in the morning of 20th October, was the rescue ship *Loch Lomond*. Her crew, and the seamen they had saved, were taken aboard the mine-sweeper *Jason*.

left: Captain D.F.G. Macintyre, who captured Germany's greatest U-boat ace, Otto Kretschmer, who would one day become Chief pf Staff to the NATO forces; right: The result of a torpedo attack on an Allied freighter.

Peter Wakker

Jack Armstrong

Tommy Howard and
Charles Bishop

bert Atkinson

below: Jack Belcher;
above: Cyril Hatton

An Allied captains convoy conference in the Second World War.

The wolfpack had dealt with HX79 as efficiently and lethally as they and their companions had dealt with SC7. By the time they had finished, thireen vessels of the convoy, including their rescue boat, were sunk. Of these Endrass and Schepke each claimed three. The formidable escort had been no more successful than SC7's on the night before, and some reasons were clear. The senior naval officer had no experience of Atlantic escort duty; there had been no meeting of the captains before the operation; the corvettes were straight out of the shipyard and their crews were inexperienced. Designed for detection under water, their Asdics received no echo from U-boats on the surface, and their depth-charges had been ineffecive. For inter-ship communication, they had relied on loud-hailers, signal lamps and flags. They had neither radar, nor any means of overhearing the U-boat's radio transmissions. As Commander Allen, Captain of HMS *Leith*, reported later: "With the present means available the difficulties of communications between the Senior Officer and other escorts . . . cannot be too highly stressed—and, as a corollary, the necessity for teamwork." Paul Lund and Harry Ludlam in their *Night of the U-Boats*, put it even more strongly: "It was a story of inadequacy, unpreparedness and grim endurance on the part of the British,

left: After a bombing raid by Allied aircraft, U-boats being built in Bremen; right: Deck gun defence.

Admiral Max Horton, C-in-C, Western Approaches, Liverpool.

and cool, rewarding enterprise by the Germans."

That same night, an outbound convoy from Britain came under attack, and another seven merchant ships went down. The destruction of thirty-eight vessels in three days and nights, at no cost to the U-boats, was a feat of arms that entirely justified Dönitz's belief in *die rudeltaktik*. It also gave rise to an urgent reappraisal in Whitehall of escort tactics, organization and equipment. For those ill-fated convoy crews it came too late. For the men who sailed the merchant ships, every passage put their lives in the balance, and most of the weight was on the other side. "Unless we get protection', one sea-

British Merchant Navy survivors of
a German Navy submarine attack.

A dance in a time out of war for these seamen in World War Two.

soned master said, "we shan't find men to crew our ships." The fact that matters never came to that is a tribute to the men who sailed with the convoys.

It was not until November 1942 that a firm British hand was laid on the progress of the Atlantic battle: Admiral Sir Max Horton was then assigned to the command of the Western Approaches. Sir Max was an able, energetic officer, and in World War I he had been a successful submariner himself; indeed, his sinking of the German cruiser *Hela* on 13th September 1914 had been the first ever of an enemy warship by a Royal Navy submarine. He also happened to enjoy a game of golf, in which it was his habit to indulge himself on most afternoons. Having played his round at Hoylake, he would return to his office at Derby House in Liverpool, work late into the night, refreshed by a continuous supply of cordials, and reappear bright and early in the morning to resume his work.

It was Horton, perhaps more than anyone, who wove the strands of anti-submarine warfare into a coherent whole, and it was he, when Karl Dönitz pulled his raiders out of the Atlantic at the end of May 1943 after the bitterest winter on record, who would send this measured signal to his ships: "The tide of the battle has been checked, if not turned. The enemy is showing signs of strain in the face of the heavy attacks by our sea and air forces."

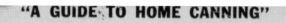

"A GUIDE TO HOME CANNING"

THE AUTHENTIC

25¢

VICTORY

COOK BOOK

Tested Recipes for
DELICIOUS DISHES in WAR TIME
VITAMINS and NUTRITIONAL
VALUES FEATURED

FOR VICTORY

AUTHENTIC PUBLICATIONS CO.   192 BROADWAY, NEW YORK

PRINTED IN U.S.A.

"We'll have lots to eat this winter, won't we Mother?"

Grow your own Can your own

500 FOOD-EXTENDER **Wartime Recipes**

Food alternatives, Rationing hints, and Economical suggestions to help you serve nutritious, attractive wartime meals

MEAT in the meal *for Health Defense*

THE *New* BOOK OF RATION-REVISED RECIPES AND MENUS Including A HANDY *Changeable* TABLE OF POINT-VALUES FOR *all* FOODS...

Coupon Cookery

by Prudence Penny

UNDER ATTACK

On 11th March 1940 Squadron Leader Paddy Delap of No 82 Squadron, RAF Bomber Command, piloting a twin-engined Bristol Blenheim, attacked a surfaced U-boat at low level in the Schillig Roads near Wilhelmshaven in the Heligoland Bight. The submarine, U-31, was hit by Delap's bombs and sank off Borkum Island. Although on that occasion she was salvaged and repaired (only to be sent down—permanently—in the Atlantic eight months later by the destroyer *Antelope*), U-31 stands as the first U-boat to be sunk by an air attack in World War II. U-320, bombed by a Consolidated PBY Catalina of Coastal Command almost five years later, was the 196th and the last to

meet death from the sky.

From the first years of the war, the RAF's heavy bombers, joined in 1942 by those of the USAAF, frequently attacked the shipyards and U-boat bases at Kiel, Hamburg, Wilhelmshaven and Bremen on the Baltic coast, and they continued to do so until Germany surrendered. Thousands of mines were laid in the approaches to the bases, and U-boats setting out on patrol or returning home, had to be shepherded by trawlers or patrol boats through the dangerous waters. As the war progressed, U-boats at sea were increasingly harried by aircraft of the Allied maritime commands.

The RAF's Fleet Air Arm had been handed over to the Royal Navy in 1938, and in December 1940, after much heart-searching, the Air Ministry had moreover decided that, although it would retain ownership and the administration of Coastal Command, operational control would pass to the Admiralty on 1st April 1941. The decision was unexceptionable, and in reaching it the Air Marshals showed a better understanding of inter-service relations than was ever exhibited by German Reichsmarschall Hermann Göring, whose philosophy was illustrated by his phrase: "Anything that flies belongs to me, and me alone." In practice, however, the British plan did not quite work out—at least not for some time. The Coastal Commander-in Chief, Air Chief Marshal Sir Philip Joubert described it as "a polite fiction", and in September 1942 he called for a single supreme control for the whole anti-U-boat campaign to co-ordinate the policies of British, Canadian and American naval and air authorities". Although it was generally agreed that such a policy was strategically desirable, if not to say essential, it was politically impossible: the post of anti-submarine Supremo was certain to fall to a British Admiral, and neither President Roosevelt nor any good American, could go along with that.

For most of the war Coastal Command was to remain the RAF's Cinderella force. Fighter and Bomber Commands had more glamour, more apparent action and a higher priority with the aircraft and armaments industries. So it was that, in the early days, with the planes available, the Coastal crews' duties lay mainly in reconnaissance—patrolling the sea lanes in search of the enemy and radioing any sightings to the Navy. Of the Command's seventeen squadrons, the majority were equipped with the twin-engined Avro Anson, dating from the early 1930s, a lovely aeroplane to fly, but slow, limited in range, and woefully short of fire-power. Only three squadrons had the sort of aircraft—the Short Sunderland and the American Lockheed Hudson— capable of patrolling the far Atlantic waters and, with their depth-charges and machine-guns, of taking the offensive against a U-boat if they should ever find one.

At least these aircraft were effec-tive in their role. In a scrap with eight Junkers 88s, a Sunderland's gunners shot three of the enemy planes down, and the big flying boat was thereafter known by German pilots as "the flying porcupine". A Hudson of 269 Squadron on patrol from Iceland on 27th August 1941, attacked U-570 with such effect that the commander, Kapitänleutnant Rahmlow, submerging in a hurry, neglected to close all the vents and hatches. The flooded batteries produced a cloud of chlorine gas; the boat promptly surfaced and a dozen choking crewmen struggled from the conning tower on to the deck. In the words of the Hudson pilot: "We thought at first they were making for their guns, so we kept our own guns going hard. They didn't like that a bit, and tried to scramble back again. The rest of the crew were trying to get out of the hatch, and they sort of met in the middle and argued it out. It was a regular shambles for a few minutes."

The pilot made low, tight turns around the U-boat, with his guns trained on the conning tower, and a piece of white material which turned out to be the commander's starched dress shirt, was waved in surrender. The Hudson's fuel was running low, and the wireless operator signalled for assistance, while the pilot circled. "Practically the whole crew", he reported, "seemed to be in the conning tower, packed in so tightly they could hardly move. We were close enough to see their faces, and a glummer-looking lot I never saw in my life." A

The virtualy bomb-proof mass of
the Bordeaux U-boat bunker.

XVIII
XVII

relay of aircraft kept watch over the prize until a destroyer arrived to escort her into port—the first U-boat to be captured intact. She was towed to Iceland, repaired, and later served the Royal Navy as HMS *Graph*. U-570's flag was presented to 269 Squadron by the Navy as a memento of the feat.

Her 1st Officer, Bernhardt Berndt, was condemned as a coward by his fellow Ubootwaffe POWs and, in an attempt to redeem his honour by escaping (with the aim of scuttling his captured U-boat at Barrow-in-Furness) was shot dead by a patrol of "Dad's Army"—Britain's Home Guard. Postwar, the unhappy Rahmlow was denied membership of the U-boat Old Comrades Association, and it is notable that in Admiral Dönitz's memoirs, which contain some reference to almost every U-boat that came under his

HMCS *Sackville*, a Canadian corvette now moored in Halifax, Nova Scotia; right: Depth-charges on the *Sackville*.

command, the fate of U-570 is not mentioned.

Meanwhile, the many hundreds of thousands of licensed private pilots in America had found themselves a role in national defence. On 1st December 1941, six days before the Japanese attack on the U.S. Navy's big ships in Pearl Harbor, they had formed the Civil Air Patrol. In the best tradition of the Minutemen of the War of Inde-

pendence, they stood by at airfields in every eastern state, ready to fly to America's defence at a moment's notice. Once General Hap Arnold was convinced of their potential, the Air Corps provided them with fuel, and Washington, somewhat grudgingly, paid the pilots $8. per day ($5. for the ground staff), out of which they had to find their own uniforms, servicing, food and accommodation.

Their service gave no exemption from the draft, and as time went on most of the younger men and women joined the armed forces, but their elders always filled the gaps. In their miscellaneous collection of red and yellow Stinsons, Fairchilds, Taylorcraft and Wacos, always flying in pairs, they patrolled the eastern seaboard at low level, up to sixty miles offshore, from dawn to dusk. They had single-channel radios, and their life jackets were inner tubes of motor tyres.

When the CAP flights had proved their worth by sighting U-boats, ships in distress, and drifting lifeboats, and reporting their positions, the big oil companies combined to make a hefty grant of cash, and the Air Corps provided 100-pound bombs and 350-pound depth-charges to be carried under the patrolling aircraft's wings. In July 1942 a Widgeon thus equipped flying out of Atlantic City, New Jersey, was the first to attack and claim the sinking of a U-boat twenty-five miles off the coast. In the eighteen months before the U.S. Navy took over all anti-U-boat warfare and confined the CAP to search-and-rescue missions, the flying Minutemen

A British depth-charge attack on a U-boat in the north Atlantic in WWII.

flew 86,685 sorties, made 173 U-boat sightings, dropped eighty-two bombs or depth-charges and claimed the destruction or damage of two U-boats. They lost ninety aircraft and twenty-six fliers. The Navy's Commander, Admiral Ernest King, recorded his appreciation of their "valuable contribution", and his staff, eschewing all effusiveness, noted their "interesting record of service".

For the airmen serving in an anti-submarine role, one highly frustrating feature was that their achievements were often impossible to assess, as was described in the official pamphlet *Coastal Command* published by His Majesty's Stationery Office in 1942: "The attack is so swift and the results, if any, so prompt that the surface of the sea has closed like a curtain too swiftly for them to be accurately perceived and recorded. Though great patches of oil have stained the sea, though bubbles have formed and burst upon it, the U-boat may not be stricken to death. It may still be able to limp back ton one of the numerous bases at its disposal for a refuge between the north of Norway and the southwest of France. On the other hand, it is equalliy possible that the opposite may have occurred and that the bombs or depth-charges have accomplished their purpose and that the U-boat went down the long slant to destruction, manned by a crew of choked and drowning men.

"Following the Sunderlands and Hudsons came the long-range American PBYs equipped with British radar and bomb-racks—together with some mid-range fighter-bombers such as the Bristol Blenheim and the Beaufighter, and the longer-range Vickers Wellington, a twin-engined bomber that was being replaced in Air Chief Marshal Harris's Bomber Command by four-engined heavies. The weapons also— new, 300-pound depth-charges, 600-pound bombs, torpedoes with acoustic homers and new, low-level bombsights, were far more effecive, and the mere sight of an aircraft turning to attack was enough to force a U-boat to submerge and so be diverted from its prey.

"Most important was the latest electronic aid—centimetric radarforty precious sets of which, recently acquired by his Command, the British bomber chief had been persuaded to transfer to the Coastal Command Wellingtons. Seated in his cabin at 10,000 feet, the radar operator could scan nearly four thousand square miles of sea, and a "blip" painted on his screen by the rotating antenna showed him the range and bearing of its source. The effect was immediate and it came as an unpleasant shock to the watch on a U-boat's bridge to see an aircraft not merely searching but heading straight towards them from over the horizon and sometimes out of heavy cloud. If an airborne radar was directed at them, they expected warning from the "Metox" detector, but this proved ineffective against short-wave transmissions of the new search radars. Many a radio report to BdU read: "Crash dive. Attack by aircraft. No radar warning."

If his U-boat were one of those

German Type VII U-boats tied up in
the port of Wilhelmshaven.

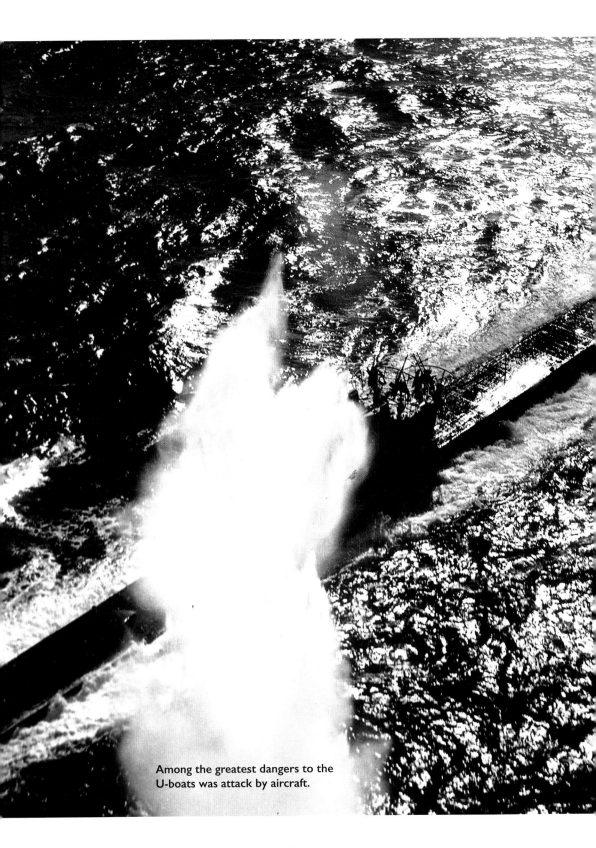

Among the greatest dangers to the
U-boats was attack by aircraft.

equipped with more and better anti-aircraft armament, a commander might decide to stay on the surface and fight it out, in which case the pilot could either reciprocate or circle out of range while calling up the nearest corvette or destroyer. If the commander opted to submerge, the aircrew, watching through binoculars, would see the first man disappearing into the conning tower, at which they would perhaps have thirty seconds in which to make their attack, with bombs, depth-charges, or torpedoes; if they were skilled enough and quick enough, they might catch the raider at its most vulnerable time.

Adapting to the threat, the U-boat commanders changed their tactics, staying down longer in the daylight hours and surfacing in darkness to launch their attacks. One of the counter-measures to the night assault was provided by the "Snowflake" rockets, fired by the ships to illuminate the scene; another, more effective one was the Leigh light (named after the RAF Squadron Leader who invented it), installed in two squadrons of Wellingtons in the late summer of 1942 and in the PBYs and B-24s when they joined the anti-submarine campaign. When the aircraft's radar found surfaced U-boat, the pilot approached it in a shallow dive and switched on the Leigh light at about 150 feet. The brilliant, broad beam, focused on the conning tower, turned the night to day, blinding the deck watch while the aircraft made its bombing run.

PBY Catalina flying boat

Norman Wilkinson

In the early years of the war, U-boats on long-range patrol were refuelled at sea by surface tankers, but by the end of 1941 all of these had been hunted down and sunk by the Royal Navy—a fate not entirely unexpected by the Kriegsmarine. In 1942, ten big Type IX U-boats were specially constructed to rearm, resupply and refuel the boats at sea and to carry medical stores and replacements for sick or wounded crewmen. The 1,600-ton "milch cows" as the Royal Navy called them, had a range of over 12,000 nautical miles and a speed of ten knots, and each carried enough diesel oil to double the endurance of five convoy raiders. There was nothing wrong with the conception, but the operational problems were formidable. To effect a rendezvous between two small vessels in the vastness of the ocean called for very skillful navigation; it also took time, while each lay on the surface, readily detectable by radar or by eye, to transfer fuel and supplies and to row or tow torpedoes from one boat to the other. Life-jackets were attached to the fuel pipe to keep it afloat, but it was liable to break of the oil were pumped too fast. The Allied air forces and navies were quick to seize upon the weaknesses and to give the U-tankers their full attention. The original ten were quickly sunk, and ten more planned for 1943 were cancelled when it became clear to BdU that the ever-growing scale of the anti-submarine campaign made the U-tanker not so much a milch

A German deck-gun crew at work; right:
British sailors firing Hedgehog weapons
at a U-boat; far right and bottom left:
Rescued U-boat crewmen.

cow as a dead duck.

On a clear night in June 1944, a few hours after the Normandy invasion had begun, a Liberator on patrol between the Scillies and Ushant found a surfaced U-boat and sank it with a perfect 'straddle' of six depth-charges, three on each side of the hull. Minutes later a second dark shape appeared against the moonlit sea. The aircrew's gunfire was was hotly returned from the U-boat's deck. The attack went on. Four depth-charges fell on the port beam and two on the starboard. The sub went down by the stern. With their bombload expended the aircrew watched anxiously. "We were just going to send a message to base," said the pilot, "hoping someone might come and finish the job, when the mid-upper gunner shouted 'She's going down. It's just like a Hollywood picture.' "

Although the operations of the Allies maritime air commands and naval air arm didn't make the headlines as often as those of the bomber and fighter commands, their long sustained contribution to the Atlantic battle was enormous. Crews of RAF Coastal Command flew 800,000 hours above the oceans, making 1,300 attacks on enemy vessels. 1,700 aeroplanes were lost in those missions, and 5,800 aircrew— including 1,600 from Britain's dominions and her European allies lost their lives while flying them.

Rescued and captured, German submariners after their ordeal at sea.

THE LAST ACT

U-94 as it arrives at its home port, St Nazaire, on 31 May 1941 with Kapitänleutnant Herbert Kuppisch in command.

Until August 1945, when two atom bombs finally convinced the Japanese that their only option in the war was surrender, it had always been accepted that wars were never won until the enemy's army was defeated in the field. In Europe three months earlier, as the soldiers of the Western Allies and the Soviet Union had converged upon Berlin, it had seemed that the axiom held good. Some questions, though, still remained. It could be argued that there might have been a different outcome if, in 1940 or 1941, Admiral Dönitz had been able to deploy the 300 ocean raiders he had wanted and been given active air support; or indeed if Hitler, frustrated by the stalemate in the west, had not turned on Russia in 1942.

Of all the factors that contributed to the Allied victory, moral and physical, military and technical,

Returned safely from another
Atlantic patrol, Korvettenkapitän
Günther Prien.

strategic and tactical, none was more important than the long campaign that kept the oceans open to traffic, without which Britain could not have survived, let alone provide the springboard for the Normandy invasion. In assessing that campaign, pride of place must go to the courage and endurance of the merchant seamen (and the fact that many were of foreign stock yet chose to risk their lives for the cause of the Western Allies, was something the U-boat men could never understand). Next in importance came the massive aid to Britain from North America in the shape of the "Cash and Carry" programme, the "Lend-Lease" package of destroyers, a squadron of Liberators and two of Flying Fortresses, the Canadian and American share in convoy duties, and the activities of the Tenth Fleet—aid reciprocated westward by Britain's years of experience in escort tactics, a fleet of armed trawlers, "Huff-Duff" (HFDF) radio and Ultra intelligence.

The third factor was the arrival, just in time, of very long-range aircraft equipped with high-tech radar, to close the mid-Atlantic gap. There was no doubting the effectiveness of radar, especially in poor visibility or when there was low-cloud, but more U-boats were detected by huff-duff and the good old human eye than by "the seeing radio" (as Henry L. Stimson, the U.S. Secretary for War, rightly called it. Dönitz and his staff, however, constantly over-estimated its importance and, ill-advised by their scientists, took precautions against it that were ineffective. It was the combination of the centimetric radar and the massive growth of air power that eventually made the surface of the seas a U-boat killing ground.

The fourth contribution was made by Commander (later Captain) Frederick John Walker. By 1943 the offensive team tactics he had evolved to beat the German wolfpacks had been adopted by the Royal Navy and by the U.S. Navy's hunter-killer groups. Walker's *Black Swan*-class sloops behaved on the ocean like a bucket in a maelstrom (even the hardiest sailor could feel queasy in a sloop), but they were highly manoeuvrable, and when in action, much like hounds on a scent; appropriately enough, it was Walker's practice to have *A Hunting We Will Go* played fortissimo on the ship's Tannoy when he sailed out of Liverpool in HMS *Starling* His No. 2 Support Group sank twenty-one U-boats, including six in the course of one operation, and he himself destroyed U-264, the first snorkel boat to put to sea.

Along with Captain Donald Macintyre, 'Johnny' Walker was recognized as the undoubted champion of anti-submarine warfare, and his efforts were acknowledged by the very rare award of the Distinguished Service Order with three bars— each the equal of another DSO. Worn out by his efforts, Walker

died shortly after D-Day at the age of forty-eight and was laid at rest at sea.

The last factor was the extremely valuable intelligence provided about U-boat movements by the cryptographers of the Government Code and Cypher School at Bletchley Park. It is probably true to say that the GC & CS played as significant a role in winning World War II as any other single unit, service or civilian.

The Signals Intelligence branch of GC & CS collected, collated and disseminated operational information obtained by eavesdropping on enemy communications."Ultra" became the code-name for intelligence resulting from the interpretation of high grade codes and cyphers. The "Sigint" people's problem was that all security-graded radio traffic within Germany's armed forces was protected by the use of a highly sophisticated enciphering machine known as *Schlussel-M* or *Enigma*. In the use of Enigma, messages were typed on an ordinary keyboard and passed through electrical circuits to three rotors, which had seperate contact points for every letter of the alphabet in a scrambled order. Each letter of the message, as the operator typed it, was transmitted in turn to the first, second and third rotors, changing each time, until the enciphered letter to be used by the operator was displayed on a screen above the keyboard and then transmitted in Morse code. At the receiving end, an operator with a similar device and a list of rotor settings for the day, simply went through the enciphering routine in reverse. As the rotors could be changed at will, and the number of electrical circuits could be increased, the variations possible verged on the infinite. The machine was compact and simple to operate, and the resulting code was virtually impenetrable.

Ultra intelligence served the British well: the position of every U-boat was plotted in the Admiralty's Submarine Tracking Room, and the shipping losses fell. Then, on 1st February 1942, the Hydra naval code was changed; not because Dönitz suspected it had been broken, but as a matter of routine, and the sinkings doubled in the three months that followed, until Ultra, (which, by now, was being shared with the Americans) came back on stream. Another grim hiatus came in the spring of 1943, when the Germans added a fourth rotor to Enigma. In the fortnight it took the crypto-analysts at Bletchley to find the answer, the wolfpacks ranged at will, and two unlucky convoys—the slow SC122 of fifty-four ships and the faster HX229 of forty, sailing from New York—suffered twenty-two losses. That slaughter was the last of the Ubootwaffe's triumphs. May 1943 was to be known in Germany as "the month of the lost U-boats". From that time on, Ultra never failed. No wonder Winston Churchill called it

The U-boat memorial near Kiel, Germany.

"the precious secret".

The U-boats were still a threat, though, to which the Allies were devoting a hundred thousand men, over forty aircraft carriers, and hundreds of destroyers, sloops and corvettes. But neither the advent of the snorkel, nor all the new gadgetry provided by German industry for the later types of U-boat towards the end of 1944, and in early 1945, could hide the writing on the wall: Germany had lost the battle for the sea lanes of the world. Although twenty-four Allied merchantmen were sunk between September and December 1944, it was at a cost of fifty-five U-boats. Brave though they were, and loyal to their Fatherland, most U-boat captains knew they were beaten, and so did their crews. Some still persisted in pressing home attacks against overwhelming odds, but others—more prudent—were content with softer targets. Though the hardships abd perils had been in vain, at least they would not end their lives, like so many of their comrades.

By June 1944, every German with the slightest notion of what was going on around him knew that the Allies were about to launch a great invasion, and that it would fall somewhere on the coast of France. Some believed that the Wehrmacht would wipe out the invaders before they got off the beaches; others that even if a few managed to get ashore, the famed Atlantic Wall could not be breached. No matter what, it was sure to come and had to be withstood. In Field Marshall Erwin Rommel's view, lose the battle for the beaches, lose the war.

As for the Kriegsmarine, Dönitz had known for some time that the few remaining surface ships had no further role in World War II. He was obliged to turn to his Ubootwaffe—indeed there was nowhere else to turn. According to his mem-

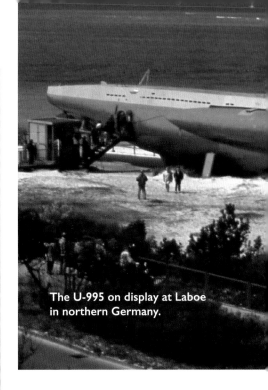

The U-995 on display at Laboe in northern Germany.

oirs, his orders included these words: "Every vessel taking part in the landing is a target of the utmost importance which must be attacked regardless of risk. Every boat that inflicts losses on the enemy while he is landing has fulfilled its function even though he perishes in so doing." It was a mark of how low the Nazi star had fallen since the days of the Blitzkrieg and "the Happy Time" that the U-boat, once one of Germany's prime weapons of attack, was to be committed, like the Luftwaffe before it, to defence.

Thirty-six of the surviving U-boats were in Bay of Biscay bunkers, with another twenty-two lying in Norwegian fiords. Fifteen of the 1st Flotilla were berthed in Brest and, on a fine May morning, the captains were told what their Admiral would require of them when

"Overlord" was launched. As Herbert Werner, who was one of those captains, described in his book *Iron Coffins*, the order was to "attack and sink the invasion fleet with the final objective of destroying enemy ships by ramming". If Werner's recollection is correct (and fellow U-boat captain Erich Topp supports it, although there are some who dispute it), the words provided one final dark analogy with the combat fliers—not, however, with the Allied bomber crews but with the Kamikaze pilots of Japan.

The captains waited grimly for their sailing orders and eventually they came at midnight on 6th June. Werner's U-415 was one of eight U-boats, none of them equipped with a snorkel, which left the harbour, escorted by trawlers and patrol boats through the inlet and out into the bay. As Werner related it the orders were to proceed at top speed on the surface to the south coast of England, and there to carry out the duties for which they had been briefed—suicidally, if need be. Two days later U-415 limped back into Brest, badly damaged—one of only three boats to survive the mission. Meanwhile, seven snorkel-fitted boats had sailed for the Baie de la Seine, but the impact they could make on the vast armada of landing craft and 800 warships was insignificant. "By 30thJune", Werner wrote, "U-boat operations since the invasion began were a full-fledged disaster. We had sunk five Allied cargo ships and two destroyers, and we had lost twenty-two U-boats."

American tanks rolled into Brittany, and the RAF pounded Saint-Nazaire, Lorient and Brest. By September Brest was under siege, encircled by the U.S. 6th Armoured Division, and the Bay of Biscay bases were no longer tenable. The remaining U-boats were sent on a hazardous six-week voyage around the coast of Ireland, through the North Channel, past the Orkney Islands and the Shetlands, harassed by aircraft and warships all the way, to anchor in Bergenfiord on the southwest coast of Norway. The contrast between Bergen's gaunt, glacial landscape, grey seas and chilling fogs, and the memory of the sunshine, pleasant promenades and cafés that had been left behind, underlined the decline in the fortunes of the U-boat arm. Although there were to be a number of determined offensive patrols in British coastal waters in the ensuing months, and one last desperate mission to the east coast of America in the spring of 1945, the retreat from France was to mark the end of the Ubootwaffe's effective part in World War II.

Berlin's communiqués continued to be highly optimistic. In September the German people were informed that a new and devastating weapon, the V-2 rocket, which even then was falling on England and would soon fall on America, was sure to make the Allies sue for peace; in December the news was that the Army's great offensive in the hills of the Ardennes was about to hurl the British and the Americans back into the sea; in February 1945 it was announced that the Führer had taken personal command of the capital's defences; in April, that the death of the American president, always Britain's friend, would result in a breach between the western Allies. The facts, however, were that the British withstood the flying bombs and rockets in the same sturdy way they had endured the Blitz, that the Ardennes offensive was halted and crushed within ten days, that Franklin D. Roosevelt was succeeded in the White House by a man no less dedicated to the defeat of Germany than he, and that the only command Hitler could exercise from his bunker in Berlin was over the immediate circle of his entourage. Just before midnight on 1st May he sombre strains of Wagner, seldom known to introduce good news, preceded a special broadcast bulletin, which included one last piece of Nazi fiction: "Our Führer, fighting to his last breath, fell for Germany in his Headquarters . . ."

At the end of World War I Germany's U-boats had been surrendered in droves, while seventy of the Kaiser's captured surface ships, in a last defiant act, had been scuttled by their crews in Scapa Flow; in 1945 Germany's sailors believed that the Nazi fleet, including the U-boat arm, should follow that example. The signal to commanders was to be the code-word Regenbogen"Rainbow", but the Grand Admiral never sent the signal. The British had stipulated that there must be no demolition and no scuttling of vessels, otherwise the bombing of strategic targets—or what remained of them—would go on. Dönitz had no choice: on 5th May 1945 he sent the order to his U-boats to transmit their positions in plain language and sail to Allied ports. "Unbeaten and unblemished", he added to the message, "you lay down your arms after a heroic fight without parallel."

Germany at that point still had a strength of over 350 U-boats, including many new Type XXIs and XXIIIs, which had never been in action. Of these, the majority were in German ports or at anchor in the fiords. Of those remaining at sea, two were sailed to Argentina by their hard case commanders, while the rest headed for Britain or America, in accordance with their orders, hoisting the black flag of piracy, which, for the occasion, was to signify surrender. Many boats, however, were commanded by men who either could not believe, or could not accept, their Admiral's last order. They exchanged signals on the old combat frequency, and word that passed between them was Regenbogen. In the waters of the Baltic and in the North Sea over 200 U-boats were scuttled by their crews.

By September 1945, 156 U-boats

The motto of Otto Kretschmer, the highest-scoring ship-killer of the German Navy, was "One torpedo, one ship down."

had been surrendered, and of those that fell into the Royal Navy's hands, 110 were either scuttled or sunk by gunfire in 300 feet of water off the coast of northern Ireland, where they remain.

From *Iron Coffins* by former U-boat commander Herbert A. Werner: "Finally the hour arrived: 2130 on April 11, 1944. My crew had assembled aboard on the aft deck. There were no well-wishers at the water front, no music, no flowers. My commands echoed hollowly in the concrete bunker. U415 sailed quietly into the shallow inner harbour, stern first, then turned and followed the nervous mine-sweeper into the long, dark channel leading into the open Atlantic. I had taken this route many times before. However, there was a great difference. I was now in command, with the lives of 58 men in my hands, at a time when our prospects for success and survival were at their lowest."

"Under the common concrete roof, the shipyard personnel worked around the clock to have the fifteen U-boats repaired, equipped and fitted out for their most vital mission. Torpedoes, fuel and food were stowed aboard simultaneously to reduce the loading period, and our machinists made scores of repairs on their own, helping to put the boats in fighting condition by the required deadline. While the activity in the shipyards slowly subsided and the invasion jitters mounted in the compound, the enemy completed his immense preparations across the English Channel. He also increased his air strikes on Biscay ports, harassing us at any hour, keeping our flak crews chained to their guns. Night after night, groups of Allied aircraft swept over our U-boat bases, seeding harbours and waterways with magntic mines. Day after day, our mine-sweepers searched for the hidden menace, and the sound of explosions echoed occasionally from the cliffs in the Bay of Brest. Large Anglo-American bomber fleets penetrated France, systematically hammering, disputing

and obliterating roads, rails, stations, depots, airfields, barracks, bridges, villages, and cities—devastating the beautiful France which had been virtually untouched by the war."

"A new day dawned hesitantly over the coast of Normandy where the greatest invasion of all time was in progress. A prodigious fleet—over 4,000 landing craft with thirty divisions of Allied troops, 800 destroyers, cruisers, battleships, warships of all sizes and classes—was about to reach the Continental shore, which was being pulverized by the bombardment of over 10,000 enemy planes. Meanwhile divisions of paratroopers rained down behind our coastal defenses and countless gliders landed laden with men, tanks, guns and supply.

"While the French soil rocked under millions of exploding bombs and grenades, while the first waves of the intruders were decimated by the concentrated fire of the defenders, while only a few hundred of our own planes found their way into the sky, while the resistance of our tanks and guns and human walls slowly crumbled under the ponderous assault from the air and the sea—while all that happened, fifteen U-boats waited under the protective cover of the concrete bunker in Brest, twenty-one more lay in other Biscay ports, and another twenty-two remained in safe Norwegian fiords.

"It was past 1700 when I re-

Rescued U-boat crewmen in captivity aboard an Allied warship.

For these German sailors, the war is truly over.

turned to the bunker. The radios had been silenced. Instead, the huge vault-like structure resounded to the songs of our 800 crewmen, who remained eager to sail again against the enemy even if it meant sailing straight to their deaths. At 2100, as night descended upon the Normandy battlefields, fifteen U-boats slipped out into the Bay. The night was clear. The stars glittered faintly in a still light sky. Soon a full moon would rise and light up our way into the Atlantic."

"While the Royal Air Force spared no effort to sink us and other lone wolves, the British Navy ignored us completely. Not a single ship entered our area. I operated precariously in the square for an entire week without seeing or hearing a destroyer or an Allied landing craft. During the ninth night of our fruitless operation, I challenged the Tommies' aircraft by signalling base: NO TRAFFIC IN AREA. SEND NEW ORDERS.

"Immediately after transmitting the message, we dived and floated at a scant twenty-five meters, awaiting Headquarters' answer. The reply instucted us to return to Brest. We made the journey back into port in just forty-two hours, hopping and floating with the rising tide into the narrows of Brest. It was late evening July 13, when we arrived at the pick-up point. A quick rise, a fast answer to the escort's challenge, and U415 made her last dash into port.

"At 2235 I manoeuvred my boat into the bunker, under the protection of a concrete ceiling seven meters thick. The engines stopped. The eery light cast dark shadows on the yellow faces of my men as Kapitän Winter walked over the gangplank. He accepted my report and welcomed the crew with a smile, but was unable to conceal his grave concern. After he had passed the files he turned toward me and said with a subdued voice, 'You've been called back to prepare for a special task. Get together with my Chief Engineer to determine the major problems, those which require immediate attention and can be taken care of quickly. You have to be equipped for patrol in three days. That's all the time we can give you' "

"I was not sorry to see July come to an end. As usual in recent months, conditions were worsening at an accelerating rate. Strong Allied forces, spreading out from Normandy against only light resistance, threatened to cut Brittany off from the rest of France, thus denying us access to Germany. Our most important U-boat bases on the Atlantic coast came under greater peril every day. These bases—the once lively ports of Brest, Lorient, and St Nazaire—were practically dead already, along with their U-boat flotillas. In July alone, eighteen more boats had been sunk, most of them by air attack. Among this number were the obsolete, Schnorkel-less U212 and U214, which had sailed from Brest to keep our front yard free of Allied naval units. British destroyers, which had begun to tighten the noose around our port, had sent the pair to the bottom."

". . . I took over the help of Marbach's boat. Most of the crew already knew me or had heard of me; and this, together with the mounting Allied threat, prompted the me to accept their new Captain with relief and with hope. Since a portion of the crew had gone on leave and presumably would be unable to return, I filled the ranks with machinists and seamen of U415, who had taken a jealous interest in my new boat. In preference to fighting on land, they would gladly have sailed a dinghy to sea to fight British destroyers.

"The days now passed rapidly in

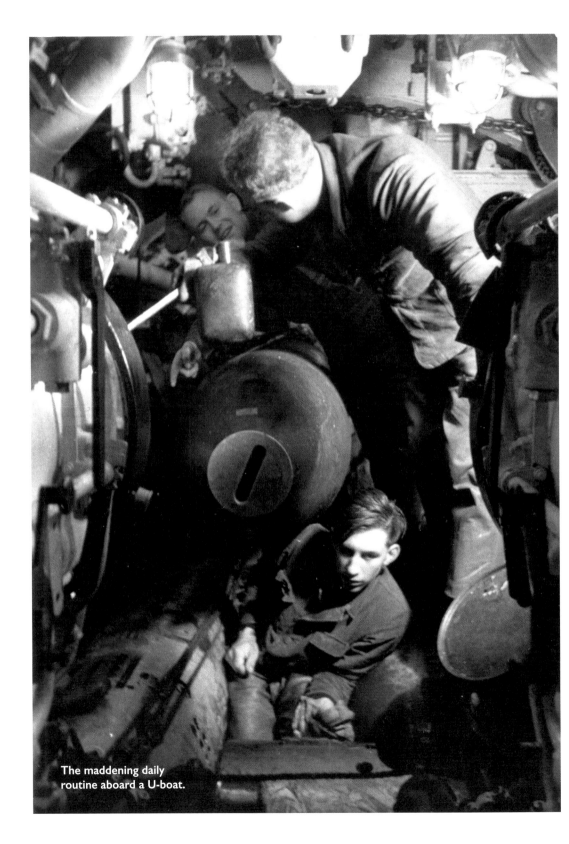

The maddening daily
routine aboard a U-boat.

preparation for our sailing. My composite crew worked desperately to beat the clock and to offset the increasing shortage of reliable, experienced shipyard personnel. More and more of our French workers were encouraged by the Allied advances to abandon their conquerors. Some of them actually ran away during lunch time. Worse, those who remained behind were more hostile than trustworthy, and they had to be watched constantly. Moreover, the remainder of my crew from U415 were sent to the outer trenches of Brest, and those left at my disposal were pestered constantly by German civil employees, who offered large bribes to be smuggled aboard when we dashed out of the trap. Under these hectic conditions, it was impossible for us to meet our sailing schedule.

"Brest awaited the enemy. More and more of our troops poured into the city as fast-moving Allied units fanned out from Normandy, threatened Paris, surrounded Lorient, and reached for St Nazaire. The citizens of Brest now stayed in their houses and waited developments with a mixture of fear, eagerness and stoicism. Too late, Headquarters ordered all U-boats to evacuate Brest, Lorient and St Nazaire. By then the British had anticipated Dönitz's command and had sealed off our escape routes. Strong destroyer forces had steamed south, surrounding and besieging the three ports. Night after night, Allied aircraft dropped their mines into navigable waters, stopping all surface traffic and making the U-boats comings and goings a fatal proposition. In addition to the hunt at sea, the Royal Air Force attacked all bases repeatedly and in great strength. The tragic remnants of a glorious Fleet that once numbered several hundred U-boats now postponed their destruction by lurking in bunkers, under cover of seven meters of concrete."

"Reaching La Pallice, I paused at the entrance to the U-boat bunker and raised my face toward the sky and the sun. I savoured that moment, knowing that I would dive that night and live in obscurity for many weeks, that I would not see the sun again until I surfaced in a Norwegian fiord after an underwater voyage of some 2,000 miles, after summer had gone or even winter would have arrived. Or I might never see daylight again . . .

"As I approached my boat, I was strangely startled by the wooden containers of fresh vegetables that stood on deck. For a moment it seemed as if nothing had changed since the days of glory when I began my service aboard U-boats. Of course, nothing was the same. Like our great land victories, our few hundred U-boats had all but vanished. But at least one would die fighting."

U.S. Army inspectors in 1945 at what is
believed to be the Brest U-bunker.

Crew members of the Type VIIA
U-29 enjoying a meal in the fresh
air of Brest where their boat is
tied up in October 1940.

PICTURE CREDITS

Photographs by the author are credited PK; photographs from the collections of the author are credited AC; photographs from the Bundesarchiv are credited BUNDES, and photographs from the National Archives of Canada are credited NAC. P2: PK, P3: PK, PP4-5: PK, P7: PK, P8: PK, P10 both: PK, P11: PK, PP12-13: PK, PP14-15: PK, PP16-17: PK, P19: AC, P20: AC, PP20-21: PK, P21: PK, PP22-23: PK, P24: PK, P25: PK, P26: PK, P27: PK, PP28-29: PK, P29: PK, P31 both: AC, PP32-33: PK, P34: BUNDES, P35: AC, PP36-37: PK, P39 top: PK, P39 bottom: PK, P40: BUNDES, P41: BUNDES, P42: AC, PP44-45: PK, P47: PK, PP48-49 all: BUNDES, P50 top both: AC, P51: BUNDES, PP52-53: PK, P54: PK, PP56-57: PK, P59: PK, P60: BUNDES, P61 right: PK, P62: PK, P63: PK, PP64-65: PK, PP66-67: BUNDES, P68: AC, P70: BUNDES, P72: AC, P74: NARA, P77: AC, P78 all: AC, PP80-81: BUNDES, P82 bottom left: AC, P82 top: BUNDES, P83: BUNDES, P84 top: AC, P84 top right: BUNDES, P84 bottom: AC, P85: BUNDES, P86: PK, P87 top: PK, P87 bottom: AC, PP88-89: BUNDES, P90 all: BUNDES, P91 all: BUNDES, P92: BUNDES, P93 both: BUNDES, P95: BUNDES, P96: AC, P97 both: BUNDES, P98 both: AC, P99: BUNDES, P100: PK, PP102-103: PK, PP104-105: PK, P105 both: PK, P106 top: AC, P107: NATIONAL ARCHIVES OF CANADA, P108: AC, P109: AC, P110: AC, P111: AC, P112: AC, P113: AC, P114: NATIONAL ARCHIVES OF CANADA, P115 top: AC, P116 all: AC, P117: BUNDES, P118: AC, P119: AC, PP120-121: courtesy anonymous contributor, P. Guy, P. Wakker, R. Atkinson, J. Belcher, C. Hatton, J. Armstrong, T. Howard, C. Bishop, PP122-123: NATIONAL ARCHIVES OF CANADA, P124 both: NATIONAL ARCHIVES OF CANADA, P125: NATIONAL ARCHIVES OF CANADA, P126: AC, P127 both: AC, PP128-129: AC, PP130-131: NATIONAL ARCHIVES OF CANADA, P131: AC, P132: AC, P133 all: AC, P134: PK, PP136-137: PK, PP138: PK, P140: AC, PP142-143: BUNDES, PP144-145: U.S. NAVY, PP146-147: N. WILKINSON, P148 top and left: BUNDES, P148: bottom right: J. Schmitz-Westerholt, PP150-151 both: U.S. COAST GUARD, PP152-153: BENDES, PP154-155: BUNDES, P156: AC, P157: PK, PP158-159 both: PK, P161: BUNDES, P163: U.S. COAST GUARD, PP164: U.S. COAST GUARD, P166: PP168-169: BUNDES.

ACKNOWLEDGEMENTS

Special thanks to Margaret Kaplan, Kate Currie and Herta Krull. Many thanks too to Pauline Allwright, Malcolm Bates, Lance Bauserman, Beverley Brannon, Horst Bredow, Geoffrey Brooks, R.M. Browning Jr., Piers Burnett, Brian Burns, Ryan Cassidy, Harry Cooper, Debby Comer, Jane Costantini, Captain A.C. Douglas, Lee Edwards, Charles Eshelman, Gary Fisher, Ella Freire, Oz Freire, Betty Hamilton, Ed Holm Franc Isla, John James, Claire Kaplan, Joseph Kaplan, Neal Kaplan, Paul Kemp, Judy McCutcheon, Richard McCutcheon, James McMaster, Tilly McMaster, Hans Milkert, Michael O'Leary, Susan Roth, Vern Schwartz, Lloyd Stovall, Mary Beth Straight, John Zinner.

BIBLIOGRAPHY

Bekker, Cajus, *The German Navy 1939-1945*, Dial Prress, 1974.

Broome, Jack, *Convoy Is To Scatter*, William Kimber, 1972.

Buchheim, Lothar-Günther, *The Boat,* William Collins, 1976.

Clancy, Tom, *Submarine*, Berkley Books, 1993.

Cremer, Peter, *U-Boat Commander,* Naval Institute Press, 1985.

Dönitz, Karl, *Memoirs,* Greenhill Books, 1990.

Gallery, Daniel, *Twenty Million Tons Under The Sea*, Regnery, 1956.

Gannon, Michael, *Operation Drumbeat*, Harper Perennial, 1990.

Gray, Edwin, *The Killing Time*, Scribners. 1972.

Guske, Heinz, F.K., *The War Diaries of U-764*, Thomas Publications, 1992.

Hickam, Homer, *Torpedo Junction*, Naval Institute Press, 1989.

HMSO, *The Battle of the Atlantic*, 1946.

Hough, Richard, *The Longest Battle*, Weidenfeld and Nicholson, 1986.

Hoyt, Edwin P., *The U-Bpat Wars*, Robert Hale Ltd., 1984.

Jackson, G. Gibbard, *The Romance of a Submarine*, J.B. Lippincott

Kaplan, Philip, *Grey Wolves*, Pen & Sword, 2013.

Kemp, Paul, *Convoy Protection*, Arms and Armour, 1993.

Neitzel, Sönke, *Die Deutschen Ubootbunker und Bunkerwerften*, Bernard & Graefe Verlag, 1991.

Lewin, Ronald, *Ultra Goes To War,* McGraw-Hill, 1978.

Lund, Paul and Ludham, Harry, *Night of The U-boats*, NEL, 1974.

Macintyre, Donald, *The Battle of the Atlantic*, Pan Books, 1961.

Margoolin, V., *Propaganda: Persuaion in World War II Art*, Chelsea House, 1976.

Mason, David, *U-boat: The Secret Menace,* Ballantine Books, 1968.

Middlebrook, Martin, *Convoy*, Penguin Books, 1978.

Morison, Samuel Eliot, *The Battle of the Atlantic, Volume One*, Little Brown, 1947.

Pitt, Barrie, *The Battle of the Atlantic*, Time-Life Books, 1977.

Robertson, Terence, *The Golden Horseshoe*, Evans Brothers, 1955.

Rossler, Eberhard, *The U-Boat*, Naval Institute Press, 1980.

Showell, Jak P. Mallmann, *Hitler's U-Boat Bases*, Sutton Publishing, 2002.

Syrett, David, *The Defeat of the German U-Boats*, U. of S. Carolina Press, 1994.

Tarrant, V.E., *The U-Boat Offensive 1914-1945*.Naval Institute Press, 1989.

Waters, John, *Bloody Winter*, Naval Institute Press, 1967.

Werner, Herbert, *Iron Coffins*, Holt, Rinehart & Winston, 1969.

Westwood, David, *The Type VII U-Boat*, Naval Institute Press, 1984.